STUDIES IN ENGLISH LITERATURE

Volume X

THE
FIERCE EQUATION

A STUDY OF MILTON'S DECORUM

by

THOMAS KRANIDAS

University of California,
Riverside

1965

MOUTON & CO.

LONDON · THE HAGUE · PARIS

Printed in The Netherlands

For

HARVEY BRUCE DENSMORE

FOREWORD

Any study of Milton which engages both the poetry and prose in such brief compass is likely to seem naive. In an era of burgeoning special studies and wisely restricted "readings", only a few scholars have made the attempt to read Milton whole or to push their special readings toward a point from which a serious reconsideration of both poetry and prose is possible.

It is partly because of the richness of recent Milton studies, and their sophistication, that I can afford to be naive. The new excitement in historical criticism, the special studies in milieu, the Yale edition of the prose works and what it represents have provided the demonstration of how much Milton is a product of his time and to be read as a seventeenth-century-Puritan-Renaissance-man-under-the-influence-of-the-Italians epic poet of England. At the same time the old new critics have steadily urged attention to the text itself. That cautious and stately non-aggression pact which A. S. P. Woodhouse and Cleanth Brooks announced more than ten years ago has been assiduously violated, but no one very seriously wants it revoked. The success of D. C. Allen's *The Harmonious Vision* and of Kester Svendsen's *Milton and Science*, to take names not involved in the preliminary critical skirmishes, suggests that new and old criticisms are both participating in the rediscovery and reestablishment of Milton.

I should like to claim the double heritage. If I started as an old fashioned new critic reading the text intensively for "paradox, ambiguity, ambivalence, levels of meaning, overtones, and undertones ... archetypal, typological, epiphanic, eschatological, rhetorical and symbolic patterns of imagery, and so forth", items cited ironically by Professor Barker in his review of Milton criticism[1] it is because I think these still interesting and exciting in themselves, and a good way to begin understanding the ideas of the poem. But as this study proceeded, I tried to relate the poems to Milton's prose works, not as one discrete artifact to another, but as ideas existing in place and time and person. I hope that my study of Milton's prose, especially of the antiprelatical tracts, reflects my concern for Milton in the context of his time. I hope that my first chapter reflects a concern for Milton's poetics in the context of a rhetorical tradition. And I hope my readings in *Paradise Lost* will seem to emerge naturally from the earlier sections of the book and not to be merely juxtaposed to them.

I began this study of Milton's decorum with a somewhat simple expectation of procedure: define the term and then apply it. But the term would not define; and its omnipresence in modern Milton studies was misleading. The importance of decorum was stressed again and again in contemporary criticism, but often the term appeared to be a sponge convenient for absorbing miscalculations in the claims for methodology. Perhaps it remains a sponge in this book, but I have tried, at least, to avoid the impression that decorum is a rule like the agreement of subject and verb.

I have divided my study into three parts. The first chapter draws heavily on standard histories of criticism, though wherever possible the primary sources have been consulted. It attempts to isolate two major faces of decorum and, perhaps a little pugnaciously, to label one "major" and one "minor", or sometimes "rhetorical". The second section examines three groups of Milton's prose writings in an attempt to deduce his concept of decorum. Though I find Milton fully conscious of both faces, and ready to use both, I see a conflict between the two in much of the prose. Milton's use of the larger decorum is sustained and consistent. His rejection of the minor decorum can result in some startling effects.

The last section of this study seeks to apply my conclusions on Milton's decorum, its unity and flexibility, to certain problems in *Paradise Lost*. I am arguing a special point, that what affects us as

[1] "Seven Types of Milton Criticism", *University of Toronto Quarterly*, 25 (1955-56), 495.

eccentric or excessive is often only a part of Milton's vision of unity, richer and more comprehensive and subtler and more daring than the one we had assigned him. If my tone becomes strident in Milton's defence it is because I feel, with Milton, that indignation is properly part of critical discourse and because the academic irony of anti-Miltonists (almost a genre in itself) seems to me to represent a kind of failure in the perception of Milton's unity. This is a partial study. It is partial to Milton and only partially adequate in its treatment of the topic. The claims for "rhetorical" decorum must come from another quarter. I am aware of a serious understatement of those claims here, but I am confident that they will be made soon and fully by someone more sympathetic toward them and more competent to explore that aspect of John Milton's radiant wholeness.

This study grew out of a dissertation submitted to the graduate faculty of the University of Washington. I am grateful to the reading committee, Professors James Hall, A. C. Hamilton, and Arnold Stein for their advice and encouragement.

My interest in Milton's decorum began in Professor Stein's graduate seminar, an ideal starting place for a study which seeks to harmonize Milton's magnificence with his violence and humor. Professor Stein's critical example has functioned steadily as a guide to this work. I am deeply grateful for his personal interest, suggestions, and encouragement throughout the writing of this book.

I have many other debts and my footnotes can not fully represent them. The brilliant intensity of Milton studies in our time has been a chief factor in the pleasure and strenuousness of writing. In addition to Professor Stein's books, the work of D. C. Allen, Arthur Barker, Douglas Bush, C. S. Lewis, Kester Svendsen, Rosamund Tuve and A. S. P. Woodhouse has represented an important part of the preparation for this work. Professors Jackson I. Cope and Howard Schultz offered suggestions on parts of the earlier version of this study that helped greatly to focus some of these perceptions.

My most personal debts are to the friends and associates who have offered aid, encouragement and advice; to my friend John Haislip of Oregon State University, who offered some valuable preliminary bibliography; to my colleagues Milton Miller and Stanley Stewart, who have read parts of the manuscript; to my students, who have afforded many of these ideas a critical hearing; to Mrs. Jane Elsdon and Miss RoseAnn Marie Morgan, who have typed this manuscript; to my mother-in-law, Mrs. Myrtle Collins, who proof-read an earlier version; to the Research Committee of the University of California at Riverside, who helped make the final stages of this manuscript possible.

My wife, Kathleen, deserves thanks for all the above reasons and more. She has inspired, criticized, supported – in short, made possible – the whole process of writing this book.

Two sections of this book, in slightly different form, have appeared in American periodicals. "Adam and Eve in the Garden: *Paradise Lost*, Book V" appeared in *Studies in English Literature*, Winter 1964; "'Decorum' and the Style of Milton's Antiprelatical Tracts" appeared in *Studies in Philology*, April 1965.

CONTENTS

I. THE BACKGROUNDS OF MILTON'S DECORUM

I

The concept of decorum is as old as criticism; it may indeed be the
first criticism. Soon after the first stirrings of Western philosophy,
Xenophanes, Heraclitus, and Pythagoras among others accuse
Homer of impropriety in depiction of the gods.[1] Pindar shows that
the accusation touched the poet when he says in the "First Olympian
Ode":

It is better for a man to speak well of the gods; he is less to blame.[2]

The blame comes when the rational ideal of godliness is violated by
local mythic and dramatic details of ungodly stealing, murder and
adultery. Decorum manifests an early concern for consistency of
character; and it manifests an early concern for the relation of
poetry to the total culture.

It is this latter aspect which Aristophanes emphasizes, even over
the first. When, in *The Frogs*, he attacks Euripides for indecorousness in his portrayal of women, it is just after he has referred to
Zeus as "the thrashed one",[3] and presented Bacchus with something
less than dignity. It is not simple inconsistency of character with

[1] Hermann Diels, *Die Fragmente Der Vorsokratiker* (Berlin, 1922), I, 59-60.
See also J. W. H. Atkins, *Literary Criticism in Antiquity* (London, 1952), I, 14.
Milton is aware of this tradition of Homer's impropriety. See his comment in
An Apology Against A Pamphlet ... in *Complete Prose Works of John Milton*
(New Haven, 1953), I, 891.
[2] Richmond Lattimore, *The Odes of Pindar* (Chicago, 1945), pp. 1 and 2. Miss
Kathleen Freeman suggests that this Ode is directly influenced by Xenophanes.
See her *The Pre-Socratic Philosophers* (Cambridge, 1946), p. 93.
[3] Aristophanes, *Comedies* (New York, 1931), II, 222.

which Aristophanes charges the tragedian; it is that Euripides does not submit his ethos, that of the play, to a higher one, that of Athens. He has rejected the responsibility of the poet toward a larger context:

AESCHYLUS: So answer me: what is it in a poet one admires?
EURIPIDES: Wise counsels, which make the citizens better.
AESCHYLUS: And if you have failed in this duty, if out of honest and pure-minded men you have made rogues, what punishment do you think is your meet?
DIONYSUS: Death. I will answer for him.[4]

Aristophanes rejects the limited sense of decorum, surface consistency of character in gods or men, and substitutes the decorum of artistic responsibility to a large philosophical or religious context.

The characteristic Greek ambivalence toward art is well established when Plato issues his decree of banishment against the poet. His general regard for art is shown in the doctrine of discourse as a living organism[5] and in his testimonies to the power and beauty of language and myth.[6] So the insistence on the proper portrayal of the gods has in many places a distinctly literary bias; most often however decorum is an ethical or religious problem rather than a literary one.

A poet ought always to represent the divine nature as it really is. And the truth is that that nature is good and must be described as such.[7]

As the *Republic* develops, Plato repudiates any representation of evil in god or man:

So these charges of ours ... will not be allowed to enact the part of a woman, old or young, railing against her husband, or boasting of a happiness which she imagines can rival the gods', or overwhelmed with grief and misfortune ... Knowledge they must have of baseness and insanity both in men and women, but not reproduce such behaviour in life or in art.[8]

---

[4]   *Ibid.*, II, 234.
[5]   Plato, *The Dialogues of Plato*, transl. by Benjamin Jowett, 4th ed. (Oxford, 1953), III, 172-173.
[6]   *Ibid.*, pp. 178-180. See also Ludwig Edelstein, "The Function of the Myth in Plato's Philosophy", *Journal of the History of Ideas*, X (Oct. 1949), 463-480.
[7]   *The Republic of Plato*, transl. and ed. by Francis MacDonald Cornford (New York, 1954), p. 71.
[8]   *Ibid.*, p. 83.

The distrust of versatility is related to the concept of proper function which lies at the heart of the *Republic*:

Ἀρετή ("virtue") is that quality in an agent in virtue of which it does its particular work well; there is no other virtue than that.[9]

This idea pervades the work. The Platonic system of ethics is rooted in the concept of efficiency. The moral terms themselves—ἀρετή, ἀγαθός, σοφία; virtue, good (the adjective), wisdom – have reference to trained intelligence or skill.[10] The prime qualification for trained intelligence is to aim at "limit" or "measure" and, having attained it, to be satisfied.[11]

This idea of a limit, up to which you try to go, is that of a standard of perfection or of rightness which you try to hit off exactly. It appears, then, that in all arts the mark of skill and understanding is that the man who has them (the σοφὸς or ἐπιστήμων) knows when that wisdom is reached. He does not, Plato says, go beyond another person who understands his art; or, as we should rather say, he does not go beyond what he knows to be the principle of his art.[12]

The classical concept of limit is crucial to this study. Between us and Milton, between us and the Greeks, lies a body of thinking which abhors the idea of limit. At least partly, our ideas of limit and decorum reflect this thinking:

There is one total misunderstanding of this idea [limit: πέρας elsewhere measure: μέτρον] which we must avoid. The modern associations of the word "limit", and sometimes those of the word "measure", are the exact opposite of those which these words had for Plato. The word limit certainly suggests to us something that stops progress, and prevents us reaching perfection in anything. The Greek association of the words, at least in the idea of limit, is that of something on the attainment of which perfection is attained; it is not that which puts a stop to progress, but that without which progress would be a meaningless process *ad infinitum*.[13]

Decorum, τὸ πρέπον, is for the Greek world of Plato, the offspring of the idea of the proper functioning of parts in a whole. Every thing has its function, dictated by its natural limits. These

9   Richard Nettleship, *Lectures on the Republic of Plato* (London, 1951), p. 35.
10 Cornford, *The Republic*, p. 30.
11 *Ibid.*, p. 33.
12 Nettleship, *Lectures*, p. 37.
13 *Ibid.*, pp. 38-39.

natural limits result in internal harmony and prepare the thing for its proper function in a larger harmony. Professor Jaeger has sketched this harmony in its broad applications:

This harmony was expressed in the relation of parts to the whole. But behind that harmony lay the mathematical conception of proportion, which, t ie Greeks believed, could be visually presented by geometrical figures. The harmony of the world is a complex idea: it means both musical harmony, in the sense of a beautiful concord between different sounds, and harmonious mathematical structure on rigid geometrical rules. The subsequent influence of the conception of harmony on all aspects of Greek life was immeasurably great. It affected not only sculpture and architecture, but poetry and rhetoric, religion and morality; all Greece came to realize that whatever a man made or did was governed by a severe rule, which like the rule of justice could not be transgressed with impunity – the rule of fitness or propriety (πρέπον, ἁρμόττον). Unless we trace the boundless working of this law in all spheres of Greek thought throughout classical and post-classical times, we cannot realize the powerful educative influence of the discovery of harmony.[14]

While Plato most certainly cares about the consistency, even the rigid consistency, of character, his most important contribution to the idea of decorum is the harmony of ideally realized parts in an ideally realized whole. There is a double pressure, then, on each part; it must be "achieved" in itself, but not beyond its function in a larger whole. The two pressures translate themselves into two views of decorum which persist throughout Western literature. One view will stress consistency of the individual part, often with heavy emphasis on the value society has already placed upon that part, and be proscriptive; the other will stress the total harmony and be resonant.

Plato and Isocrates had suggested the theory of styles when they claimed that all utterance should be suited to the hearer and when they stressed the need for propriety or fitness to both subject and occasion.[15] But it is Aristotle who made concern with decorum overtly "a means of rendering statements more plausible, and hearers (or readers) more readily convinced of their truth". In a sense Aris-

[14] Werner Jaeger, *Paideia: The Ideals of Greek Culture*, transl. by Gilbert Highet (New York, 1943), I, 163-164.
[15] Plato, *Dialogues*, III, 179-180; R. C. Jebb, *The Attic Orators from Antiphon to Isaeus* (London, 1876), II, 101, 129, 132.

totle distils and makes available and usable a Platonic concept with which he agrees; or to use Milton's phrase, the Peripatetics "doe rather distinguish then deny"[16] Platonic concepts.

The brilliance of Aristotle's precepts and the extraordinary freshness of his practical advice in the two literary handbooks perhaps obscure some of the larger issues. Aristotle is a classifier of enormous skill, moving from his initial distinguishing of three classes of rhetoric[17] to those remarkable portraits of the Young Man, the Old Man, the Man in his Prime.[18] The precepts will often become quite specific:

The use of Maxims is appropriate only to elderly men, and in handling subjects in which the speaker is experienced. For a young man to use them is – like telling stories – unbecoming...[19]

Aristotle distinguishes between poetry and prose,[20] and of course, in the *Poetics*, between genres. But he works from a basic definition of style:

Style to be good must be clear, as is proved by the fact that speech which fails to convey a plain meaning will fail to do just what speech has to do. It must also be appropriate...[21]

In the passage often cited as the birthplace of the concept of Decorum, in Chapter 7 of Book III of the *Rhetoric*, we find this definition of τὸ πρέπον:

Your language will be *appropriate* if it expresses emotion and character and if it corresponds to its subject. 'Correspondence to subject' means that we must neither speak casually about weighty matters, nor solemnly about trivial ones...

This aptness of language is one thing that makes people believe in the truth of your story; their minds draw the false conclusion that you are to be trusted from the fact that others behave as you do when things are as you describe them...

Each class of men, each type of disposition, will have its own appropri-

---

[16] *Complete Prose Works of John Milton*, ed. by several hands (New Haven 1953-), II, 314. Hereafter cited as Yale *Prose*, with volume and page number.
[17] *The Rhetoric and Poetics of Aristotle*, ed. by Friedrich Solmsen (New York, 1954), pp. 31-32.
[18] *Ibid.*, pp. 121-126.
[19] *Ibid.*, p. 137.
[20] *Ibid.*, p. 166.
[21] *Ibid.*, p. 167.

ate way of letting the truth appear. Under 'class' I include differences of age, as boy, man, or old man; of sex, as man or woman; of nationality, as Spartan or Thessalian.[22]

It is true that Aristotle prepares the way for the dogmatists, just as it is true that he is aware of the possible corrupt uses of language. But it is also clear that throughout the work he subordinates the appropriateness of details to the broad idea of style as clear and appropriate.

In an important statement on the *Rhetoric*, G. L. Hendrickson has said of decorum:

It is clear that here was a principle of style based upon a general philosophical thought and as definite in its formulation as the nature of the subject allowed. There is but one conception of good writing, as of right conduct, viz. the μεσότης. But it is in no sense a doctrine of uniformity. On the contrary, individualism is its dominant characteristic, as truly as in the case of moral virtue. The differentiating modifying element is τὸ πρέπον which has many aspects...[23]

For Aristotle, τὸ πρέπον is of such central importance as to be indentified with the mean, the terms τὸ μέσον, τὸ μέτριον, τὸ πρέπον being, according to Professor Hendrickson, almost interchangeable terms.[24] But decorum is no rigid ideal:

The conception of the appropriate as consisting in a constant adaptation to environment (subjective and objective) and hence as pulsating, so to speak, within the legitimate limits of contraction and relaxation (ἐπισυστελλόμενον καὶ αὐξανόμενον τὸ πρέπον) is widely diffused in post-Aristotelian literature of artistic theory.[25]

Professor Hendrickson's comments ought to suggest one major caution in our application of the concept of decorum. No matter how central decorum is to the work of art, no matter how long the tradition of its importance, it is appplied anew to every piece of discourse, it adapts constantly to the environment; and the metaphor of contraction and relaxation ought to enforce the idea of discourse as a dynamic construct.

---

[22] *Ibid.*, p. 178.
[23] G. L. Hendrickson, "The Peripatetic Mean of Style and the Three Stylistic Characters", *American Journal of Philology*, XXV (1904), 136.
[24] *Ibid.*, p. 132.
[25] *Ibid.*, p. 135.

Aristotle is the source but not the originator of the Types of Style, the Unities, and decorum as restricted to character. These "Rules" assuredly play a part in a larger concern, but Aristotle's decorum not only avoided the rigidity of the Rules of later times, but even opposed to this rigidity the concept of an organic, "pulsating" principle of organic discourse:

> The Aristotelian doctrine of the mean could never have tolerated the definition of types of style in the sense of the χαρακτῆρες λέξεως conceived of as types of individualism. For every character of style there was but a single and universal precept, σαφῆ εἶναι [to be clear] as an indispensable prerequisite, modified and corrected by the essential artistic consideration καὶ πρέπουσαν [and appropriate].[26]

From Aristotle and through Theophrastus' lost work "On Style" comes the initial division of language πρὸς τὰ πράγματα and πρὸς τὸν ἀκροατήν.[27] The first is with regard to the subject, "language as an objective colorless medium for the statement of fact or the expression of thought"; the second is with regard to the audience, "language as a means of conveying (in addition to or as a part of the abstract thought) the color of the speaker's emotion or artistic feeling to his audience".[28] The Stoic doctrine of style developed from the first and emphasized correctness and purity of idiom, clearness, brevity and appropriateness.[29] But the appropriateness was not the broad consideration of style which Aristotle proclaimed but the appropriateness of the single word to the object (πρέπον δ'ἔστι λέξις οἰκεία τῷ πράγματι).[30]

Aristotle's insistence on clarity and propriety together as requirements of all style had been shattered into two styles each of which had different primary requirements.

It is not only with the Stoics that the strong cohesive criticism of Aristotle is weakened. Hellenistic poetics and rhetoric expressed more interest in the minor decorum of petty detail than in the major

---

²⁶ *Ibid.*, p. 136. See also Hendrickson's "The Origin and Meaning of the Ancient Characters of Style", *American Journal of Philology*, XXVI (1905), 249-290.
²⁷ Hendrickson, "Origin and Meaning", 254.
²⁸ *Ibid.*
²⁹ *Ibid.*, 258-259. Cf. Aristotle's *Poetics*, chapter 22.
³⁰ *Ibid.*

decorum of organic unity. Professor Atkins lists among the concerns of Alexandrian criticism the partaking of a meal twice within the hour in the *Iliad* IX, 222.[31] This concentration on the search for anachronism, then as now, represents a shrinkage in the quality and scale of criticism from the kind of statement Aristotle could make near the end of the *Poetics:*

Any impossibilities there may be in [the poet's] description of things are faults. But from another point of view they are justifiable, if they serve the end of poetry itself ... it is a lesser error in an artist not to know, for instance, that the hind has no horns, than to produce an unrecognizable picture of one.[32]

Hellenistic criticism in general was more concerned with the horns than with the hind. Attention to decorum became attention to detail, to minor consonances of behavior and style.

A notable example of scholastic rhetorics of the Hellenistic period, and one whose enormous later influence it is difficult for us to understand, is the *Ad Herennium*, the first treatise to formulate the three styles – grand, middle, and plain. In this work, long attributed to Cicero, there is an observable constriction and ossification of great issues:

Let us now see what qualities should characterize an appropriate and finished style. To be in fullest measure suitable to the speaker's purpose such a style should have three qualities: Taste (elegantiam), Artistic Composition, and Distinction.

Taste makes each and every topic seem to be expressed with purity and perspicuity. The subheads under Taste are Correct Latinity and Clarity.[33]

Here propriety and clarity are not prime, equal and united requisites. They are superseded by a diminished decorum, a surface propriety, *elegantiam*.

Cicero's awareness of decorum is of a higher sort. He makes a determined effort to win back oratory from false Hellenistic standards to classical, in part through his attempt to re-enlarge the concept of decorum:

[31]   Atkins, *Literary Criticism*, I, 190.
[32]   Solmsen, *The Rhetoric and Poetics of Aristotle*, pp. 260-261.
[33]   Cicero, *Ad C. Herennium: De Ratione Dicendi (Rhetorica ad Herennium)*, transl. by Harry Caplan (= *The Loeb Classical Library*) (London, 1954), p. 269.

In an oration, as in life, nothing is harder than to determine what is appropriate. The Greeks call it τὸ πρέπον; let us call it *decorum* or "propriety" ... the same style and the same thoughts must not be used in portraying every condition in life, or every rank, position or age, and in fact a similar distinction must be made in respect of place, time and audience. The universal rule, in oratory as in life, is to consider propriety. This depends on the subject under discussion, and on the character of both the speaker and the audience.[34]

Parenthetically in the same paragraph Cicero makes an interesting distinction (one which Milton, I believe, would disallow):

... for by right we indicate the perfect line of duty which every one must follow everywhere, but "propriety" is what is fitting and agreeable to an occasion or person.[35]

Cicero is no minor rhetorician; but history took the distinction between right and propriety and placed the emphasis where Cicero's sentence placed it – on propriety. Just as Aristotle's requirements had become separated among his followers, so right and propriety here are subtly disjoined. This is more clearly apparent in the comment on the two kinds of gracefulness where Cicero distinguishes a general gracefulness that is the property of all virtue and a "special ... which is defined to be a gracefulness so adapted as to exhibit propriety and sweetness under a certain elegant appearance".[36] For Plato and for Aristotle there are Rules and The Rule as for Cicero. But with the latter the emphasis is less on the final cohesiveness and comprehensiveness of the concept of decorum than on its elegant appearance. Cicero's concept is "a practical, workman-like one, with the rhetorician's eye never removed from the calculated effect on a large audience", Professor Stein has commented, but "it is too dependent on a considerateness (*verecundia*) for public opinion, and that is a kind of negative nephew (bidding us not offend) of a negative justice (bidding us not injure)".[37] Ironically, history took Cicero's early works (the *De Inventione* and *Topica*) and the spu-

[34] Cicero, *Brutus* and *Orator*, transl. by G. L. Hendrickson and A. M. Hubbell (= *The Loeb Classical Library*) (Cambridge, Mass., 1952), pp. 357-361.
[35] *Ibid.*, p. 361.
[36] Cicero, *Cicero's Three Books of Offices or Moral Duties*, transl. by Cyrus R. Edmonds (New York, 1871), p. 49.
[37] Arnold Stein, *Heroic Knowledge* (Minneapolis, 1957), p. 21.

rious *Ad Herennium* most seriously of his works on writing;[38] this emphasis makes it even easier for Cicero to be used proscriptively through much of the Renaissance. But even in the major statements on decorum, those in *Orator, De Oratore, Brutus,* and *De Officiis,* there is a constriction of scope and a loss of flexibility from the grand statements of Plato and Aristotle.

What Coleridge called the "unmethodical miscellany"[39] of Horace's *Art of Poetry* exerted an enormous influence on European criticism. Horace's theories of imitation, "the kinds" and decorum were widely adopted. With Horace "indirectly began the reign of authority and rule, as well as the constriction of literature in accordance with pre-established schemes of the past".[40] It is difficult to vault over this question of influence to an assessment of the work itself. But William K. Wimsatt, Jr. and Cleanth Brooks seem right in pointing to "the great difference in ethical and metaphysical resonance between the *Ars* of Horace and the *Poetics* of Aristotle or the *Phaedrus* of Plato".[41] The resonance and radiant harmony are not here, though many of the rules of that harmony are:

The excellence and charm of arrangement ... consists in this, – to say at each and every time just what should at that time be said.
    Each particular *genre* should keep the place allotted to it.
    If the actor's words be not in keeping with his fortune, the Roman gentry will laugh jeeringly, and the commoners too.
    ... we must always give attention to what belongs and is fitting to each age.[42]

There are dicta on violence, the number of acts, the relevant and limited function of the chorus in drama; and there are specific comments on how to portray Achilles, Medea, Ino. Fragmented, the

---

[38]   See the unpubl. diss. (St. Louis University, 1959) of Sister Mary Grace Schonlau, "A Study of the Language of Eloquence and the Principles of Decorum, Verisimilitude, and Imitation in the Plays of George Chapman".
[39]   Quoted in Allen H. Gilbert, *Literary Criticism: Plato to Dryden* (New York, 1940), p. 125.
[40]   Atkins, *Literary Criticism In Antiquity,* II, 102.
[41]   William K. Wimsatt, Jr. and Cleanth Brooks, *Literary Criticism: A Short History* (New York, 1957), p. 94.
[42]   James Harry Smith and Edd Winfield Parks, *The Great Critics* (New York, 1939), p. 115.

dicta on decorum, on the integrities of genres, seem a collection of
rules by a craftsman. This is not Platonic or Aristotelian decorum,
despite the range and the wit. The doctrine, though it does not contradict itself, lacks the organicism and unity of its great statements.
It is, like Cicero's decorum, a "negative nephew".
Post-classical criticism expresses a continuing regard for decorum,
even a primary regard. But the decorum itself has become a
concern for the "kinds". When Dionysius of Halicarnassus speaks
of the sources of a beautiful style he lists "melody, rhythm, variety,
and the appropriateness [τὸ πρέπον] demanded by these three".[43]
But the emphasis is on the *styles* and even where the metaphor of
harmony arises (in the description of the harmoniously blended or
εὔκρατον style) it is a *blended* harmony, not a radiant and unified
one. This is a matter of emphasis again, and one not easily demonstrated; but the distinction between decorum as a practical guide
to the shaping of a given piece of discourse and decorum as a philosophical idea of lively and radiant unity ought by now to be clear.
The kinds begin to dominate criticism, and decorum, constantly invoked and universally respected, begins to mean pretty clearly adherence to the rules of characterization, to the rules of the three (or
four)[44] styles, and to the rules of genre. Good and interesting criticism is written (like that of Tacitus and Demetrius) but the level of
intensity, "of ethical and metaphysical resonance", has dropped
radically. And nothing demonstrates this so well as the constriction
of the concept of decorum – from Style to Styles, from Unity to the
Unities. Even a major figure like Quintilian will participate in this
constriction of the term and will dissociate the practical use from
the intense and ideal; and in the century after Quintilian, rhetoric
moves in the direction of "perfumery, euphuism, Asiatic conceit".[45]

[43] Dionysius of Halicarnassus, *On Literary Composition*, ed. and transl. by W.
Rhys Roberts (London, 1910), p. 121. Elsewhere in the treatise, Dionysius uses
the word μέτριον in much the same sense. See also Dionysius' *The Three Literary Letters*, transl. by W. Rhys Roberts (Cambridge, 1901), esp. pp. 13, 18,
114, 115.
[44] *Aristotle The Poetics* "*Longinus*" *On The Sublime Demetrius On Style* (= *The
Loeb Classical Library*) transl. by W. Hamilton Fyfe and W. Rhys Roberts
(Cambridge, Mass., 1953), p. 257.
[45] Wimsatt and Brooks, *Short History*, p. 103.

II

It is somewhat easier to telescope medieval considerations of decorum, partly because the basic definitions have been already laid in classical times. In addition, the literary tradition, though a great one, is not a broadly theoretical one,[46] and the chief critical influences tended to be second-rate ones. The great critical writings of antiquity were lost to the middle ages. Cicero was known by immature or falsely attributed work. Quintilian was used in an attenuated way. The New Sophistic was dominant, "a revival of the artificial stylistic effects of the early Greek sophists",[47] and poetry was limited by rhetoric. Attention was paid to the importance of *ethopoeia*, to the necessity of adapting words and style to differences of age, sex, and rank, but it was a mechanical and arid regularity under the exercise of *prosopopoeia*. *Prosopopoeia* "emphasized decorum or propriety to the person speaking, the person spoken to, and to the emotional coloring of the attendant circumstances".[48] In his description of these "grammar school aids", Donald Lemen Clark has argued the value of this kind of training for a poet like Milton.[49]

If a relatively arid and limited concept of decorum persists in the schools, the interest in language of the Church Fathers provides some lively commentary. Despite Tertullian's "What has Athens to do with Jerusalem?" the classical traditions toward language are carefully examined for usefulness. Even Tertullian and Augustine, in the midst of attacking classical literature, invoke Plato. In a letter to Gregory the Wonder-worker, Origen writes:

I should like to see you use all the resources of your mind on Christianity and make that your ultimate object. I hope to that end you will take from Greek philosophy everything capable of serving as an introduction to Christianity and from geometry and astronomy all ideas useful in ex-

[46] *Ibid.*, p. 140.
[47] *Ibid.*, pp. 12-18.
[48] Donald Lemen Clark, *John Milton at St. Paul's School* (New York, 1948), pp. 242-243.
[49] *Ibid.*, pp. 206, 244-245. Professor Clark points out that though Milton's use of these "grammar school aids" decreased as he matured, this exercise of *prosopopoeiae* may, in some measure, account for the superiority of the speeches Milton composed for his characters.

pounding the Holy Scriptures; so that what ... philosophers say of geometry, music, grammar, rhetoric and astronomy – that they assist philosophy – we too may be able to say of philosophy itself in relation to Christianity.[50]

So it is the examples of rhetorical decorum which help Origen explain the doctrine of accommodation:

When divine Providence intervenes in human affairs, it uses human ways of speaking and thinking. If we have to talk to a two-year-old, we use the sort of language that children can understand, for they cannot possibly understand what we say to them unless we put aside our grown-up dignity and condescend to their way of speaking. We must suppose that God does the same when he deals with mankind and that he did so particularly when mankind was still in its childhood.[51]

This is the classic Christian statement of language πρὸς τὸν ἀκροατήν. St. Augustine devotes Book IV of his *Christian Instruction* to this concept of rhetorical decorum Christianized:

Since persuasion both to truths and falsehoods is urged by means of the art of rhetoric, who would venture to say that truth, in the person of its defenders, ought to stand its ground, unarmed, against falsehood...[52]

Indeed, Augustine is very much concerned with arguing appropriateness πρὸς τὸν ἀκροατήν. But first he must establish the decorum of decorum, so to speak, for the ministers of God.

---

[50]   Quoted in Jean Danielou *Origen*, transl. by Walter Mitchell (New York, 1955), p. 16.
[51]   *Ibid.*, p. 281. Professor C. A. Patrides identifies the *locus classicus* of this theory of accommodation as Augustine's statement in *De Civitate Dei*: "Gods anger is no disturbance of mind, in him, but his judgement assigning sinne the deserved punishment: and his revolving of thought is an unchanged ordering of changeable things: for God repenteth not of any thing he doth, as man doth: but his knowledge of a thing ere it be done, and his thought of it when it is done are both alike firme and fixed. But the Scripture without these phrases cannot instil into our understandings the meaning of Gods workes nor terrifie the proud, nor stirre up the idle, nor exercise the inquirers, nor delight the understanders. This it cannot do without declining to our low capacities". The passage, from p. 565 of John Healey's translation (London, 1610), is cited in C. A. Patrides, "*Paradise Lost* and the Theory of Accommodation", *Texas Studies in Literature and Language*, V (Spring, 1963), 59-60.
[52]   Saint Augustine, "*Christian Instruction*" in *The Fathers of the Church*, II (New York, 1947), p. 169.

A certain kind of eloquence is more fitting for youth, and another is more becoming for old age; so much so that we should not call it eloquence if it is not appropriate for the person of the speaker. There is a kind of eloquence, then, which is becoming for men eminently worthy of the highest authority and manifestly inspired by God.[53]

Using Genesis 37 ff. as example Augustine writes:

Not by human effort were these words devised; they have been poured forth from the mind of God both wisely and eloquently, so that wisdom was not bent upon eloquence, nor did eloquence separate itself from wisdom ... let us admit that our canonical writers and teachers were not only wise, but truly eloquent, with such an eloquence as was appropriate for persons of this kind.[54]

The careful separation of eloquence for the sake of eloquence from eloquence naturally bound to wisdom is like Aristotle, but the strictures on decorum are available from the Bible:

A man who has been assigned the position of teacher in the Church should keep before his eyes these three epistles of the Apostle. Do we not read in the first Epistle to Timothy: 'Announce and teach these things?' ... Is not the following admonition also found there: 'Do not rebuke an elderly man, but exhort him as you would a father?' ... There is also found this passage: 'Preach the word, be urgent in season out of season: reprove, entreat, rebuke with all patience and teaching'.... He also says in the same Epistle: 'But do thou speak what befits the sound doctrine: that elderly men be reserved,' and so on... Consequently, what are we to think? Does the Apostle contradict himself, declaring that teachers are formed by the operation of the Holy Ghost, while he himself gives them directions about what and how they are to teach?[55]

Augustine answers immediately:

The benefits of teaching applied by a human being are a help to the soul when this benefit is ordained by God who could have transmitted the Gospel to man even "not from men nor by man".[56]

This is, then, clear justification of the three traditional aims of oratory and of the traditional vehicles for attaining these three aims:

[53]   *Ibid.*, p. 175.
[54]   *Ibid.*, p. 187.
[55]   *Ibid.*, pp. 199-200. Augustine's citations are from 1 Timothy 4.11; 1 Timothy 5.1; 2 Timothy 4.2.
[56]   Augustine, *Christian Instruction*, pp. 200-201.

He will be eloquent, then, who, in order to teach, can speak about trivial subjects in a subdued style; in order to please, can discuss ordinary subjects in a moderate style; and in order to persuade, can treat of noble subjects in a grand style.[57]

There are in this work some very practical suggestions on discourse, suggestions on varying the style to keep from boring, on the right kind of introduction, on the right styles for various insensibilities.[58] But he comes back for warning on the ends of discourse, with special concern about the moderate style, whose end could be only pleasure in the beauty and elegance of the speech.

So it happens that we use even the adornment of the moderate style, not ostentatiously, but discreetly, not satisfied with merely pleasing the listener, but laboring rather for this end, that by reason of his being pleased he may be helped even to the good of which we are anxious to persuade him.[59]

There remain two points of special relevance to Milton, and they occur together in Augustine as they do in Milton. One point is the use of the grand style without shame; the other is the upright poet. The student of the *Pro Se Defensio* finds these words suggestive:

A teacher ... expresses himself without shame, not only in the subdued and moderate style, but even in the grand style, because he lives uprightly.[60]

And if the speaker cannot speak eloquently or wisely,

let him live in such a way that he will not only prepare a reward for himself but will also furnish an example to others. And let his beauty of life be, as it were, a powerful sermon.[61]

Without claiming a comprehensive examination of Augustine's attitudes toward language, we can still stress his roots in classical rhetoric and the extraordinary importance that decorum played in

---

[57] *Ibid.*, p. 201.
[58] *Ibid.*, pp. 222, 223, 225.
[59] *Ibid.*, 226-227.
[60] *Ibid.*, p. 237.
[61] *Ibid.*, cf. Milton's comments on the Orator in "The Seventh Prolusion", Yale *Prose* I, 288-289, and see his comments on Poet as "true Poem" in Yale *Prose*, I, 890 and see below, pp. 70, 94.

theories of language, Christian as well as pagan. Augustine insists that language can be used richly and variously; he insists that language adjusts to the situation. Most importantly he insists that the end of language is to teach the word of God.

There is no dearth of examples of the minor aspects of decorum in the Middle Ages. Decorum is associated with the three kinds of poetry,[62] with gentleness in speech and conduct,[63] with the occasion,[64] and the golden mean.[65] Matthew of Vendome can prescribe decorum in the description of gardens, women, and seasons, turning to the *Ad Herennium* for precepts.[66] Geoffrey of Vinsauf's decorum will reserve flowers of speech for serious themes and plainness for the comic.[67] Roger Bacon assumes the three styles[68] and Wyclif attacks the *pomposam eloquentiam* of the grammarians and insists on a simple style adapted to the hearers.[69] Decorum is summoned again and again and in different guises. Rarely does medieval literary theory suggest for decorum the burning unity and flexibility of classical statements.

It is, perhaps, not merely self-indulgent to examine Chaucer's attitude toward decorum, to measure the distance between the poet's assumption of decorum in his work and the poet's isolation and definition of a critical term. Surely Chaucer uses decorum as a basic norm against which his comedy, from the most exquisite ironies to archetypal prattfalls, is played. The comedy of the Wife of Bath, indeed of the whole marriage group, is dependent upon the traditional background of a woman's and a man's place. The fine-wire irony of the Prioress, and of Sir Thopas – these are examples of the norm made stereotype then mortally assailed in one way or another. But Chaucer, in addition makes formal critical comments on decorum. In the *Boethius* Philosophy says

---

[62]   Atkins, *English Literary Criticism*, pp. 31, 43.
[63]   *Ibid.*, p. 36.
[64]   John of Salisbury, *Metalogicon*, transl. by Daniel D. McGarry (Berkeley, 1955), p. 58.
[65]   Atkins, *English Literary Criticism*, p. 75.
[66]   *Ibid.*, pp. 192-193. Cf. Horace, *Ars Poetica*, ll. 114-127, 155-178.
[67]   *Ibid.*, p. 110.
[68]   *Ibid.*, p. 133.
[69]   *Ibid.*, p. 149.

But natheles, yif I have styred resouns that ne ben nat taken from withouten the compas of the thing of which we treten, but resouns that ben bystowyd withinne that compas, ther nys nat why that thou schuldest merveillen, sith thou hast lernyd by the sentence of Plato that nedes the wordis moot be cosynes to the thinges of whiche thei speken.[70]

And in Book II of the *Troilus* Pandarus advises on the proper love letter:

> Towchyng thi lettre, thou art wys ynough.
> I woot thow nylt it dygneliche endite,
> As make it with thise argumentes tough;
> Ne scryvenyssh or craftily thow it write;
> Biblotte it with thi teris ek a lite;
> And if thow write a goodly word al softe,
> Though it be good, reherce it nought to ofte.
>
> For though the beste harpour upon lyve
> Wolde on the beste sowned joly harpe
> That evere was, with alle his fyngres fyve,
> Touche ay o streng, or ay o werbul harpe,
> Were his nayles poynted nevere so sharpe,
> It sholde maken every wight to dulle,
> To here his glee, and of his strokes fulle.
>
> Ne jompre ek no discordant thyng yfeere,
> As thus, to usen termes of phisik
> In loves termes; hold of thi matere
> The forme alwey, and do that it be lik;
> For if a peyntour wolde peynte a pyk
> With asses feet, and hede it as an ape,
> It cordeth naught, so nere it but a jape.[71]

Chaucer makes the classic author's defense-on-the-grounds-of-decorum in the General Prologue:

> But first I pray yow, of youre curteisye,
> That ye n'arette it nat my vileynye,
> Thogh that I pleynly speke in this mateere,
> To telle yow hir wordes and hir cheere,
> Ne thogh I speke hir wordes proprely.
> For this ye knowen al so wel as I,

---

[70]   *The Poetical Works of Chaucer*, ed. by F. N. Robinson (Cambridge, 1933), p. 417 (Book III, Prose 12). Cf. "The Manciple's Tale", ll. 207-210.
[71]   Robinson, *Chaucer*, p. 482 (ll. 1023-1043).

> Whoso shal telle a tale after a man,
> He moot reherce as ny as evere he kan
> Everich a word, if it be in his charge,
> Al speke he never so rudeliche and large,
> Or ellis he moot telle his tale untrewe,
> Or feyne thyng, or fynde wordes newe.
> He may nat spare, althogh he were his brother;
> He moot as wel seye o word as another.
> Crist spak hymself ful brode in hooly writ,
> And wel ye woot no vileynye is it.
> Eek Plato seith, whoso that kan hym rede,
> The wordes moote be cosyn to the dede.
> Also I prey yow to foryeve it me,
> Al have I nat set folk in hir degree
> Heere in this tale, as that they sholde stonde.
> My wit is short, ye may wel understonde.[72]

And in the Clerk's Prologue, there is mention of the styles, with some suggestion of ossification of the high style. The host addresses the clerk:

> Telle us som myrie tale, by youre fey!
> For what man that is entred in a pley,
> He nedes moot unto the pley assente.
> But precheth nat, as freres doon in Lente,
> To make us for oure olde synnes wepe,
> Ne that thy tale make us nat to slepe.
> Telle us som murie thyng of aventures.
> Youre termes, youre colours, and youre figures,
> Keepe hem in stoor til so be that ye endite
> Heigh style, as whan that men to kynges write.
> Speketh so pleyn at this tyme, we yow preye,
> That we may understonde what ye seye.[73]

This detailed interest in the colors of rhetoric and the proliferation of genres co-existed with blurring and thickening of genres.[74] Chaucer's Monk gives a notable example of this bluntness:

> Tragedie is to seyn a certeyn storie,
> As olde bookes maken us memorie,
> Of hym that stood in greet prosperitee,

---

[72] *Ibid.*, p. 27 (ll. 725-745).
[73] *Ibid.*, p. 121 (ll. 9-20).
[74] Wimsatt and Brooks, *Short History*, p. 151. Wimsatt here uses *decorum* chiefly in respect to genre; indeed he uses the plural form *decora*.

> And is yfallen out of heigh degree
> Into myserie, and endeth wrecchedly.
> And they ben versified communely.[75]

Chaucer is a great poet who wrote great poetry; no one accuses him of lacking resonant and radiant harmony. But his concept of decorum does; it consists of details of consistency often tending to the banal (as in the Monk's definition of tragedy) and does not affirm that these details are parts which make up a whole. As such he represents the two faces of decorum in a curious way, one which fortunately does not flaw the poetry.

We can leave medieval treatments of decorum with this impression of a limited theoretical statement and still assume a fulfilled aesthetic practice. We can still deduce a literary theory from practice and perhaps we should end noting with Wimsatt and Brooks the Thomistic

basic assumption of radical harmony between man the knower and the external universe which he knows... The beauty of a beautiful object consists not merely in a self-enclosed character – but in a corresponding external relation of fitness to the knowing subject, a relation of knowability. All knowledge of the beautiful, and pleasure in the beautiful, arise by a kind of union between subject and object.[76]

The theological emphasis on unity, from Plotinus through Aquinas, finds its chief literary expression in "the aesthetic of Platonic and Biblical luminosity ... and the aesthetic of numerical and musical harmony".[77] Though Aquinas' literary comments are casual, the *claritas* of Dante's *Paradiso* is like that of Milton's Paradise in its luminosity and complex unity.

III

The Renaissance approaches the problems of literary criticism with gusto. What has been received and rediscovered is argued and reargued with extraordinary passion. Decorum is still a term with two faces – one the rigid proscriptiveness of the Rules, the other

[75] Robinson, *Chaucer*, p. 226 (ll. 1973-1982).
[76] Wimsatt and Brooks, *Short History*, p. 127.
[77] *Ibid.*, p. 139.

the resonant principle of dynamic unity. By the middle of the fifteenth century, the Ciceronian controversy provided a demonstration of the two faces. On the one hand, the Ciceronians argue for one model of propriety, the unity of conformity. Joachim Camerarius puts it strongly:

> To one fixed example and one form let the mind and eye be directed and this example and form I should wish to be the books of Cicero. I consider these ancient classics the best and any departure from them I count disgraceful, or turning to others worthy of censure.[78]

Against the single model, Pico the younger argues that "there are varying authors each approved in his own style",[79] and Erasmus addresses himself to the same problem in his powerful and influential *Ciceronianus*:

> The fact itself convinces us that no one can speak well unless he wisely withdraw from the example of Cicero. Wherever I turn I see things changed, I stand on another stage, I see another theater, yes, another world. What shall I do? I, a Christian, must speak to Christians about the Christian religion. In order that I speak fittingly, shall I imagine that I am living in the age of Cicero ... and shall I borrow words, figures, rhythms from the orations which Cicero delivered in the Senate?[80]

In his concluding speech, Erasmus is fervently aware of the threat of secular and pagan influence:

> Nor will the speech of any one seem charming which is not in accord with his character and not accommodated to the subject in hand; that will seem unnatural too which treats of a sacred theme in secular language and which contaminates a Christian theme with pagan baubles ... He who is so much of a Ciceronian that he is not quite a Christian is not even a Ciceronian because he does not speak fittingly, does not feel deeply those things of which he speaks; lastly he does not present his religious beliefs with the same adornment with which Cicero presented the philosophy of his times. The liberal arts, philosophy, and oratory are learned to the end that we may know Christ, that we may celebrate the glory of Christ.[81]

---

[78]   Quoted in Izora Scott, *Controversies over the Imitation of Cicero* (New York, 1910), I, 103.
[79]   Pico's letter to Bembo, in Scott, *Controversies*, II, 6.
[80]   *Ibid.*, II, 62.
[81]   *Ibid.*, III, 129.

This is not unlike that other celebration of decorum in *Of Education*;[82] Erasmus' conception is no more purely literary than Milton's. The problem for each is that "I, a Christian, must speak to Christians about the Christian religion". No decorum is valid which ignores the fact of Milton or Erasmus as Christian; no group of classical rules *in vacuo* is acceptable. Erasmus' living decorum adjusts to the present with that kind of systolic action which Aristotle describes. The decorum of the Ciceronians is, in comparison, a dead thing, circumscribing and faulting its ideas with the rigidity and bulk of its formal commitments.

The doctrine of accommodation and its concomitant, an emphasis on historical and literal study of texts, is another contemporary aspect of decorum and most influentially stated by John Colet:

Moses after the manner of a good and pious poet ... was willing to invent some figure, not altogether unworthy of God, if only it might but be profitable and useful to men; which race of men is so dear to God, that God himself emptied himself of glory, taking the form of a servant,that he accommodate himself to the poor heart of man. So all things of God, when given to man, must needs lose somewhat of their sublimity, and be put in a form more palpable and more within the grasp of man.[83]

At the fountainhead of the English Renaissance stand the Oxford Reformers, asserting this liberal doctrine of accommodation, pressing for liberty and purity at once against religious and rhetorical "orthodoxy". Sir Thomas More strikes against both orthodoxies in the *Utopia*.

"That is what I was saying", replied he, "that there is no room for philosophy in the courts of princes".

"Yes there is", said I, "but not for this speculative philosophy that makes everthing to be alike fitting at all times: but there is another philosophy that is more pliable, that knows its proper scene, accommodates itself to it, and teaches a man with propriety and decency to act that part which has fallen to his share. If when one of Plautus's comedies is upon the stage and a company of servants are acting their parts, you should come out in the garb of a philosopher, and repeat out of 'Octavia' a discourse of Seneca's to Nero, would it not be better for you to say nothing than by mixing things of such different natures to make an impertinent

---

[82] Yale *Prose* II, 366-367. And see below, Chapter II.
[83] Quoted in Frederic Seebohm, *The Oxford Reformers* (London, 1896), pp. 56-57.

tragi-comedy? For you spoil and corrupt the play that is in hand when you mix with it things of an opposite nature, even though they are so much better ... It is even so in a commonwealth and in the councils of princes ... you are not obliged to assault people with discourses that are out of their road, when you see that their received notions must prevent your making an impression upon them. You ought rather to cast about and to manage things with all the dexterity in your power so that if you are not able to make them go well they may be as little ill as possible..."[84]

It is significant that the Oxford brand of decorum moves easily between theology and rhetoric, between daring heresy on the one hand and daring popularisation on the other. The concept of decorum is meaningful only as a whole. This decorum is dynamic and pulsating, but it can stop (as Milton does in the *Samson* preface) to make a contemptuous reference to tragi-comedy. The Oxford decorum is not essentially concerned with genres, the kinds of style, or character types, though it is richly traditional with roots in Origen, Macrobius, Pseudo Dionysius, and the Florentine Academy. The reformers reject Ciceronianism and stratified allegorical interpretation. In their insistence on relating literary decorum to religious and philosophical decorum, to a total harmony, they are closer to the classical sources and to Milton than are the literary law-givers of Italian criticism.

More's attack on speculative philosophy ought to make one other point clear. The persistence of a major tradition of decorum need not mean strict homogeneity or identical attitudes towards Plato or Cicero or anyone else. A part of this major tradition of unity is its flexibility; a part of its flexibility is the ease with which it revaluates the uses of the parts.

The rediscovery of Aristotle, Quintilian, and Longinus resulted in "a Renaissance of furious theoretical activity"[85] during the sixteenth century in Italy. The continuity and weight of this activity has been a major concern of modern Renaissance scholarship and continues to be.[86] Our glimpse at it will stress only the two aspects of decorum we have identified as important to this study.

[84]   In *Ideal Commonwealths*, ed. by Henry Morley, 8th ed. (London, 1899), pp. 56-57.

[85]   Wimsatt and Brooks, *Short History*, p. 156.

[86]   Standard sources include J. E. Spingarn, *Literary Criticism in the Renaissance* (New York, 1949) and *Critical Essays of the Seventeenth Century* (Bloom-

The fundamental problem of this criticism was to justify imaginative literature, and Aristotle's *Poetics* provided excellent answers to critics.[87] Involved with the justification were the issues of the imitation of life in poetry, and the function of poetry; stemming from them was the question of decorum. The Renaissance concept of decorum, Professor Spingarn has said, "may start from either of two points of view".[88] The first may be seen as a transposition, by Horace and after him the Renaissance critics, of Aristotle's tentative distinctions of character from the *Rhetoric* to the domain of poetry. The second "necessitated the maintenance of the social distinctions which formed the basis of Renaissance life and of Renaissance literature". Here Spingarn limits the concept of decorum to the depiction of character. But he seems to recognize the restrictiveness of this decorum and notes a loss of "something of the profundity and the universality of the highest art".[89]

It is true that in its commonest Renaissance usage decorum does refer to the depiction of character. We can see in Trissino's *Poetica* the elaborate division of emotions (after Aristotle's *Rhetoric*) which led to character stereotype, the decorum of rigid character definition.

Of those who have been injured, and enemies, and adversaries, the choleric and free are less to be feared than are the mild, and two-faced, and malignant, because it cannot be known when such as these are about to act and when they are far from it.[90]

But in Giraldi Cinthio's lengthy statement, we have more than character involved:

The poet should ever have his eye on decorum which is nothing else than what fits places, times and persons ... the ancient observers of the nature of things say that decorum was that beauty, that grace, which springs

---

ington, 1957); Allen Gilbert, *Literary Criticism: Plato to Dryden* (New York, 1940); Vernon Hall, *Renaissance Literary Criticism* (Gloucester, Mass., 1959).
[87]   Spingarn, *Literary Criticism*, p. 18.
[88]   *Ibid.*, p. 86.
[89]   *Ibid.*, p. 87. Vernon Hall Jr. emphasizes this social aspect in his *Renaissance Literary Criticism*. See esp. pp. 57-63, 128-140, 208-214. For Milton's admittedly different emphasis see pp. 185-189.
[90]   In Gilbert, *Literary Criticism*, pp. 219-220.

from the forms of speech that are joined together with judgement and with measure and carry with them some exposition of characters, which should shine out in words just as the beauty of color shines out in a beautiful body. In short decorum is nothing other than the grace and fitness of things and should be considered not merely in actions but also in the speeches and answers of men among themselves...[91]

Again we are aware of the dual nature of decorum. And again emphasis is important. Cinthio's suggestion that decorum permeates a work emphasizes the whole, while listing the parts. In other critical statements the listing of parts can dominate the whole.

It is with Cinthio that the dramatic unities begin to convert into laws. Cinthio promulgates the unity of time, Maggi the unity of place.[92] But the first clear formulation is in the *Poetica* of Castelvetro, one of the three Italians mentioned by Milton as teachers of the "sublime art" of poetics. In what seems a perverse reordering of values, Castelvetro makes the unity of action an expedient of the requirements of time and place.

In comedy and tragedy, there is usually one action not because the fable is unfitted to contain more than one action, but because the restricted space in which the action is represented and the limited time, twelve hours at the very most, do not permit of a multitude of actions.[93]

This is an example of the restrictiveness of Italian Renaissance criticism, rich as it is in energies and ambitions. The disparagement of Homer (criticism of the Nausicaa incident on the grounds of decorum appears again and again),[94] a preference for the decorum of Seneca over the Greeks,[95] the rigid and minutely detailed requirements for types of character (i.e. decorum by age and profession)[96] – these are part of the legacy of Italian criticism.

Though tending to rigidity in character decorum and in the unities, certain of the Italians were more liberal in considering genres. The reason was the existence in their midst of the enormously popu-

---

[91] *Ibid.*, pp. 272-273. For Cinthio's other views on decorum see pp. 249, 261 and 273 n.
[92] Spingarn, *Literary Criticism*, p. 91, p. 93.
[93] *Ibid.*, p. 100.
[94] For example, in Giraldi Cinthio and Tasso. See Gilbert, *Literary Criticism,* pp. 261, 298.
[95] *Ibid.*, p. 249.
[96] Spingarn, *Literary Criticism*, p. 88.

lar *Orlando Furioso* of Ariosto and the *Orlando Innamorato* of Boiardo. Written before Aristotle's canons began to dominate Italian criticism, the two romances clearly violated epic precepts, in many eyes successfully. Cinthio, Pigna, and Tasso defend the romance against Speroni, Minturno and others,[97] but the most important immediate effect was the attempt by Torquato Tasso to reconcile the epic and romantic forms in his *Discourses on the Heroic Poem* and by example in the *Jerusalem Delivered*.[98] The generic minutiae are not here explicitly related to decorum. Rather, in the *Discourses*, Tasso utilizes the term *decorum* in the sense of proper depiction of custom and the rigid depiction of character:

> Things then that depend on custom, as the manner of jousting, the customs of sacrifices and banquets, ceremonies, the decorum and dignity of persons can, I believe, be arranged as befits the customs that exist and rule the world today. It would therefore be unfitting to the majesty of our times that the daughter of a king, with her maiden companions, should go to wash clothes in the river, yet in the time of Nausicaa, told of by Homer, it was not deserving of reprehension... But the things that in themselves are good do not have any regard for custom nor does the tyranny of convention extend over them in any respect.[99]

Tasso cites Ariosto as excelling "in the propriety of action and the decorum of persons",[100] but it is in the limited sense of a "tyranny of convention", within an art that is "fixed and determined". Mazzoni, the third Italian mentioned by Milton, cautions the poet in "depicting wicked customs with the words of his own mouth... It then appears from reason and authority that the poet does not sin in morality by imitating wicked customs if he adds to them the punishment they deserve..."[101]

A final notice of Italian usage of decorum can be given in Guarini's *The Compendium of Tragi-comic Poetry* (1601). It is a defense of his *Il Pastor Fido*. Here again Italy produces a liberal attitude

[97]   *Ibid.*, pp. 108-124.
[98]   *Ibid.*, p. 119. The *Jerusalem Delivered* was the center of critical activity during the last half of the century. The critical pressure was persuasive enough to elicit from Tasso a revision of the poem along classical principles. See Spingarn, *Literary Criticism*, p. 122 and Gilbert, *Literary Criticism*, p. 466.
[99]   Gilbert, *Literary Criticism*, p. 498.
[100]   *Ibid.*, p. 499.
[101]   *Ibid.*, pp. 398, 400.

toward genres. Tragi-comedy is superior according to Guarini because it "does not inflict on us atrocious events and horrible and inhumane sights, such as blood and deaths, and ... on the other hand, does not cause us to be so relaxed in laughter that we sin against the modesty and decorum of a well-bred man".[102] Tragedy, Guarini writes, "will have great characters, true names, a serious action, and magnificent manners, stage appliances, decorum, language and ideas".[103] But arguing against the sadness which tragedy leaves, he asks "what need have we today to purge terror and pity with tragic sights, since we have the precepts of our most holy religion, which teaches us with the word of the gospel?"[104] The end of tragi-comedy is to mingle "all the tragic and comic parts that can coexist in verisimilitude and decorum, properly arranged in a single dramatic form with the end of purging with pleasure the sadness of the hearers". [105] One eye here is on the box office. And we feel in one place that decorum is a kind of stage property, in another a kind of cliché invoked but completely subordinated to the pleasure-purge.

One cannot deny the significance of sixteenth century Italian criticism. The struggle of these men towards a new classicism and an independent dignity for literature was to influence deeply two hundred years of continental and English literature. And the debts of Milton to these critics are abundantly documented. But in terms of a dynamic concept of decorum, in terms of abrasive but nourishing contact with the living literature of England, the Italian classicists are of less interest to our purposes than the quieter but more central tradition of Christian humanism flowing through the Oxford Reformers. English criticism follows the Italians, and Sidney is a celebrated case, but there is in Renaissance English poetry, including Jonson and Milton, no slavish adherence to the dramatic unities, genres, or character decorum of Italian criticism.

For the Elizabethans, the term *decorum* has something of the Protean quality of the term *wit*. The best critics, like Puttenham, are aware of the instability of the term. Curiously, the acknowl-

[102]   *Ibid.*, p. 512.
[103]   *Ibid.*, p. 521.
[104]   *Ibid.*, p. 523.
[105]   *Ibid.*, p. 524.

edged ambiguity of the term does not prevent dogmatism in the claims made for one aspect.

As a unifying master concept, decorum is related to, or at least contiguous to, Ascham's idea of the εὐφυής man:

> He that is apte by goodnes of witte, and appliable by readines of will, to learning, having all other qualities of the minde and partes of the bodie, that must an other day serve learning, not trobled, mangled, and halfed, but sounde, whole, full, and hable to do their office.[106]

For the Elizabethans, G. Gregory Smith has argued, decorum "is identical with what has been understood as proportion, 'decency', the truly euphuistic..."[107] Ascham can plead for wholeness[108] and at the same time for "perfect imitation of classical authors".[109]

> Bicause the providence of God hath left unto us in no other tong, save onelie in the Greke and Latin tong, the trew preceptes and perfite examples of eloquence, therefore must we seeke in the Authors onelie of those two tonges the trewe Paterne of Eloquence...[110]

Few single commentaries will demonstrate this wide spread between the flexible and rigid ideas of unity, but that spread well represents the general Elizabethan attitude.

The ubiquity and instability of the term is seen in any examination of standard Elizabethan critical documents. When Gascoigne (*Certayne Notes of Instruction*, 1575) mentions decorum it is in the sense of stylistic or generic consistency:

> For as to use obscure and darke phrases in a pleasant Sonet is nothing delectable, so to entermingle merie jests in a serious matter is an *Indecorum*.[111]

But Gabriel Harvey makes the marginal note in his copy of Gascoigne, "A *non sequitur*".[112] Harvey thinks of indecorum in specific terms of character, as does Whetstone in *The Dedication to Promos and Cassandra*:

---

106 In G. Gregory Smith, *Elizabethan Critical Essays* (London, 1904), I, 1.
107 *Ibid.*, I, xli.
108 *Ibid.*, I, 6. I have modernized 'u's' and 'v's', 'i's' and 'j's'.
109 *Ibid.*, I, xlii.
110 *Ibid.*, I, 22.
111 *Ibid.*, I, 48.
112 *Ibid.*, I, 359.

Manye tymes (to make mirthe) they make a Clowne companion with a Kinge; in theyr grave Counsels they allow the advise of fooles; yea, they use one order of speach for all persons: a grose *Indecorum*, for a Crowe wyll yll counterfet the Nightingale's sweete voice; even so affected speeche doth misbecome a Clowne.

I devided the whole history into two Commedies, for that, *Decorum* used, it would not be convayed in one.[113]

In 'E. K.'s' *Epistle Dedicatory to the Shepheards Calender* there is praise of the 'New Poet's'

dewe observing of Decorum everye where, in personages, in seasons, in matter, in speach; and generally, in al seemely simplycitie of handeling his matter and framing his words...[114]

But Richard Stanyhurst is probably referring to character only when he speaks of Virgil "with eeche *decorum* so duely observed..."[115] The greatest Elizabethan critical document provides the most dramatic contrast. Sidney's *Apologie* speaks of a kind of imitation which suggests a harmony of Platonic intensity:

For any understanding knoweth the skil of the Artificer standeth in that *Idea* or foreconceite of the work, and not in the work it selfe.[116]

But, notoriously, it is those passages which complain of the violation of the dramatic unities and criticize the mixing of genres and characters which most overtly represent Sidney on decorum.[117]

Another influential treatise, William Webbe's *A Discourse of English Poetrie* (1586) avoids the term though it mentions in several places the synonyms "decency", "fitness" and "propriety".[118] There is perhaps some attempt to minimize the word itself. Webbe uses it in its larger sense only when he quotes 'E. K.';[119] in the translation of Horace's *Ars Poetica* which he annexes to his *Discourse*, Webbe uses Decorum but once, and in a limited way:

In a *Satyr* greate heede is to be taken of the place, of the day, and of the

---

[113] *Ibid.*, I, 59-60, 58.
[114] *Ibid.*, I, 128.
[115] *Ibid.*, I, 137.
[116] Smith and Parks, *The Great Critics*, p. 195.
[117] *Ibid.*, pp. 225-227.
[118] G. Gregory Smith, *Elizabethan Critical Essays*, I, 238, 247, 248, 252, 256, 273, 275.
[119] *Ibid.*, I, 263.

personnes: as of *Bacchus*, *Silenus*, or the *Satyres*. Againe of the unmeetnesse or inconvenience of the matter, and of the wordes that they be fitted according to the persons: of *Decorum*, that he which represented some noble personage in the Tragedie bee not some busy foole in the *Satyr*: finallie of the hearers, least they be offended by myxing filthy matters with jestes, wanton toyes wyth unhonest or noysome with merry thinges.[120]

Elsewhere in the translation from Horace he uses "propriety",[121] "τὸ ὁμαλόν, that is equallie",[122] "τὸ ἁρμοστόν, which is interpreted *convenientiam*, fitnesse: as it is meete and agreeable every where a man to be stoute, a woman fearefull, a servant crafty, a young man gentle".[123]

The major Elizabethan statement on decorum is in George Puttenham's *The Arte of English Poesie* (1589). Although references to decorum (or decency) are scattered throughout the work, it is in the third book, "Of Ornament", that we find an extended discussion. Puttenham is conscious of the instability of the term, but he proceeds to make comprehensive and suggestive claims for it:

In all things to use decencie, is it onely that giveth every thing his good grace & without which nothing in mans speach could seeme good or gracious, in so much as many times it makes a bewtifull figure fall into a deformitie, and on th' other side a vicious speach seeme pleasaunt and bewtifull: this decencie is therfore the line & levell for al good makers to do their busines by. But herein resteth the difficultie, to know what this good grace is, & wherein it consisteth, for peradventure it be easier to conceave then to expresse... the mynde for the things that be his mentall objectes hath his good graces and his bad, whereof th' one contents him wondrous well, th' other displeaseth him continually, no more nor no lesse then ye see the discordes of musicke do to a well tuned eare. The Greekes call this good grace of every thing in his kinde τὸ πρέπον, the Latines *decorum*; we in our vulgar call it by a scholasticall terme *decencie*; our owne Saxon English terme is *seemelynesse*, that is to say, for his good shape and utter appearance well pleasing the eye; we call it also *comelynesse*... This lovely conformitie, or proportion, or conveniencie, betweene the sence and the sensible hath nature her selfe first most carefully observed in all her owne workes, then also by kinde graft it in the appetites of every creature working by intelligence to covet and desire, and in their actions to imitate & performe; and of man chiefly before any other crea-

120   *Ibid.*, I, 294.
121   *Ibid.*, I, 290.
122   *Ibid.*, I, 292.
123   *Ibid.*

ture as well in his speaches as in every other part of his behaviour ... the election is the writers, the judgement is the worlds ... it may be a question who shal have the determination of such controversie as may arise whether this or that action or speach be decent or indecent ... so as he who can make the best and most differences of things by reasonable and wittie distinction is to be the fittest judge or sentencer of *decencie*... But by reason of the sundry circumstances that mans affaires are, as it were, wrapt in, this *decencie* comes to be very much alterable and subject to varietie...[124]

This is an effort to define the word in its broadest sense, while remaining conscious of the difficulties of criteria. Puttenham's examples are considerably less effective than his precepts; but the chapter as a whole suggests something of the scope and flexibility of Aristotle's decorum.

In the *Preface* to his 1591 translation of *Orlando Furioso*, Sir John Harington has some amusing comments to make which touch decorum. The first is a complaint which would indicate that there existed a good deal of bad criticism based on a superficial kind of decorum:

But sith we live in such a time, in which nothing can escape the envious tooth and backbiting tongue of an impure mouth, and wherein everie blind corner hath a squint eyed *Zoilus* that can looke a right upon no mans doings (yea sure there be some that will not sticke to call *Hercules* himselfe a dastard, because forsooth he fought with a club and not at the rapyer and dagger), therefore I thinke no man of judgement will judge this my labour needlesse...[125]

Elsewhere, Harington uses decorum as a kind of minimal guard against the charge of obscenity:

There is so meet a decorum in the persons of those that speake lasciviously, as any of judgement must needs allow ... yet me thinks I can smile at the finesse of some that will condemn him [Ariosto], and yet not onely allow but admire our *Chawcer*, who both in words & sence incurreth far more the reprehension of flat scurrilitie, as I could recite many places, not onely in his millers tale, but in the good wife of Bathes tale, & many more, in which onely the decorum he keepes is that that excuseth it and maketh it more tolerable.[126]

[124]   *Ibid.*, II, 173-175.
[125]   *Ibid.*, II, 194-5.
[126]   *Ibid.*, II, 215.

From "line & levell for al good makers to do their busines by" to protective device against the charge of obscenity: this is the range of the term among the Elizabethan critics.

Criticism chooses, at the turn of the century, to fight some of its battles in and about the theater. Earlier, in the Prologue to his *Damon and Pithias* (1571), Richard Edwards had preached:

The old man is sober; the young man rash; the lover triumphing in joys;
The matron grave; the harlot wild, and full of wanton toys:
Which all in one course they no wise do agree,
So correspondent to their kind their speeches ought to be.
Which speeches, well-pronounc'd, with action lovely framed –
If this offend the lookers on, let Horace then be blamed,
Which hath our author taught at school, from whom he doth not swerve,
In all such kind of exercise *decorum* to observe.[127]

Later Jonson becomes champion. In the Prologue to *Every Man in His Humor* (acted 1598), he seems to be attacking Shakespeare directly.

To make a child, now swaddled, to proceed
Man, and then shoot up, in one beard and weed,
Past threescore years; or with three rusty swords,
And help of some few foot-and-half-foot words,
Fight over York and Lancaster's long jars,
And the tiring-house brings wounds to scars.
He rather prays you will be pleas'd to see
One such to-day, as other plays should be;
Where neither chorus wafts you o'er the seas,
Nor creaking throne comes down the boys to please

But deeds and language such as men do use
And persons such as comedy would choose
When she would show an image of the times,
And sport with human follies, not with crimes.[128]

and in *Volpone* (1605):

And so presents quick comedy refined,
As best critics have designed;
The laws of time, place, persons he observeth,
From no needful rule he swerveth.[129]

---

[127] Joseph Quincy Adams, *Chief Pre-Shakespearean Dramas* (Boston, 1924), p. 572, ll. 19-26.
[128] In Hazelton Spencer, *Elizabethan Plays* (Boston, 1933), p. 255.
[129] *Ibid.*, p. 302.

In *Every Man Out of His Humor* (1600) Jonson demonstrates his flexibility and argues for the evolution of comedy:

And though that in him [Aristophanes] this kind of poem appeared absolute and fully perfected, yet, how is the face of it changed since! in Menander, Philemon, Cecilius, Plautus, and the rest, who have utterly excluded the chorus, altered the property of the persons, their names, and natures, and augmented it with all liberty, according to the elegancy and disposition of those times wherein they wrote. I see not then, but we should enjoy the same license or free power to illustrate and heighten our invention as they did; and not be tied to those strict and regular forms which the niceness of a few, who are nothing but form, would thrust upon us.[130]

And in the address "To the Readers" prefixed to *Sejanus* (1605), he again argues for freedom from classical precept:

First if it be objected that what I publish is no true poem in the strict laws of time, I confess it; as also in the want of a proper chorus, whose habit and moods are such and so difficult as not any whom I have seen since the ancients (no, not they who have most presently affected laws) have yet come in the way of. Nor is it needful or almost possible in these our times and to such auditors as commonly things are presented, to observe the old state and splendor of dramatic poems with preservation of any popular delight... In the meantime if in truth of argument, dignity of persons, gravity and hight of elocution, fullness and frequency of sentence, I have discharged the other offices of a tragic writer, let not the absence of these forms be imputed to me...[131]

Despite the flexibility demonstrated in the last two quotations, Jonson was remembered by Dryden as "a painful observer of τὸ πρέπον or the *decorum* of the stage". Dryden remembers too that Jonson "used extreme severity in his judgment on the incomparable Shakespeare for the same fault".[132] Perhaps some of the intransigence of the reputation came from *Timber* where Jonson describes propriety:

Words are the Peoples, yet there is a choise of them to be made. For *Verborum delectus origo est eloquentiae.* They are to be chose according

---

[130]   Gilbert, *Literary Criticism*, pp. 537-538.

[131]   *Ibid.*, pp. 538-539. Compare Lope de Vega and his similar defense of comedies which violate the rules in order to please the audience; see Gilbert, pp. 541-548.

[132]   John Dryden, *Essay on Dramatic Poetry*, in Gilbert, *Literary Criticism*, p. 633.

to the persons wee make speake, or the things wee speake of. Some are of the Dampe, some of the Councell-board, some of the Shop, some of the Sheepe-coat, some of the Pulpit, some of the Barre, & c. And herein is seene their Elegance and Propriety, when wee use them fitly, and draw them forth to their just strength and nature by way of Translation or *Metaphore*.[133]

For all his historical reputation as a kind of iron-bound classicist, Jonson recognized the evolution of literary forms. Jonson's flexibility (as well as his admiration for Bacon) shows in this comment:

Nothing is more ridiculous then to make an Author a *Dictator*, as the schooles have done *Aristotle*. The dammage is infinite knowledge receives by it. For to many things a man should owe but a temporary beliefe, and a suspension of his owne Judgement, not an absolute resignation of himselfe, or a perpetuall captivity. Let *Aristotle* and others have their dues; but if wee can make farther Discoveries of truth and fitnesse then they, why are we envied?[134]

It is wise to remember this statement of Jonson's when we read his far more often quoted criticisms of Sidney and Donne and Guarini:

That Sidney did not keep a decorum in making every one speak as well as himself.
    That Done's Anniversaire was profane and full of blasphemies: that he told Mr. Done, if it had been written of the Virgin Marie it had been something...
    That Guarini, in his Pastor Fido, kept not decorum, in making Shepherds speak as well as himself could.[135]

The case of Jonson is in several ways an example of distances between theory and practice. And John Webster is measuring these distances when he defends himself against the charge of violating the critical laws, in his Preface to *The White Devil* (1612):

If it be objected this is no true Dramaticke Poem, I shall easily confesse it; *non potes in nugas dicere plura meas Ipse ego quam dixi*; willingly and not ignorantly, in this kind have I faulted; for should a man present to such an Auditory the most sententious Tragedy that ever was written, observing all the critticall laws, as heighth of stile and gravety of person, inrich it with the sententious *Chorus*, and, as it were, life 'n Death in the passionate and waighty *Nuntius*; yet, after all this divine rapture, *O dura*

[133]   Spingarn, *Critical Essays*, I, 37.
[134]   *Ibid.*, I, 43.
[135]   "Conversations of Ben Jonson with William Drummond of Hawthornden", in Spingarn, *Critical Essays*, I, 210-211, 212.

messorum ilia, the breath that comes from the uncapable multitude is able to poison it; and ere it be acted, let the author resolve to fix to every scene this of *Horace,*

> *Haec hodie Porcis comedenda relinques.*[136]

Though Webster includes "M. Shake-spear"[137] among those by whose light he wishes to be read, it is generally assumed that Shakespeare is the quiet receiver of attacks from the decorous-minded. There is evidence though that Shakespeare himself consciously exploits the term with a harsh or broad comic effect. The word itself appears only three times in the plays – in all three cases the scene is one which *lacks* ordinary social decorum:

> Now, as fond fathers,
> Having bound up the threatening twigs of birch,
> Only to stick it in their children's sight
> For terror, not to use, in time the rod
> [Becomes] more mock'd than fear'd; so our decrees,
> Dead to infliction, to themselves are dead,
> And liberty plucks justice by the nose,
> The baby beats the nurse, and quite athwart
> Goes all decorum.
>
>   (*Measure for Measure* I, iii, 23-31)[138]

Iras: Amen. Dear Goddess, hear that prayer of the people! for, as it is a heart-breaking to see a handsome man loose-wiv'd, so it is a deadly sorrow to behold a foul knave uncuckolded; therefore, dear Isis, keep decorum, and fortune him accordingly!

>   (*Antony and Cleopatra* I, ii, 73-78)[139]

> *Cleo*: If your master
> Would have a queen his beggar, you must tell him
> That majesty, to keep decorum, must
> No less beg than a kingdom.
>
>   (*Antony*, V, ii, 15-18)[140]

In the first case, decorum is brought in sardonically to emphasize its loss: decorum itself "goes athwart". In *Antony*, the concept oper-

[136] *Ibid.,* I, 65.
[137] *Ibid.,* I, 66.
[138] *The Complete Plays and Poems of William Shakespeare,* ed. by William Allan Neilson and Charles Jarvis Hill (Boston, 1942), p. 396.
[139] *Ibid.,* p. 1248.
[140] *Ibid.,* p. 1282.

ates within a metaphor that turns upside down all normal propriety. All three cases, though in two different ways, emphasize the loss of hierarchy; it is interesting that the term should appear in contexts which suggest just that loss in at least partially comic terms.

There are at least two other references to decorum (not by name). In *Twelfth Night*, Malvolio breaks in upon the caterwauling of Sir Toby, Sir Andrew, and Festo:

Mal. My masters, are you mad, or what are you? Have you no wit, manners, nor honesty, but to gabble like tinkers at this time of night? Do ye make an alehouse of my lady's house, that ye squeak out your coziers' catches without any mitigation or remorse of voice? Is there no respect of place, persons, nor time in you?

(II, iii, 93-99)[141]

The last sentence, of course, could be directly transplanted from a treatise on decorum. The satire here explicitly foreshadows Malvolio's attempt to violate decorum by making love to his mistress. And the ridicule of generic divisions and the dramatic unities is apparent in Polonius':

The best actors in the world, either for tragedy, comedy, history, pastoral, pastoral-comical, historical-pastoral, tragical-historical, tragical-comical-historical-pastoral, scene individable, or poem unlimited.

(*Hamlet*, II, ii, 415-419)[142]

It is not unjust, I think, to conclude this brief survey of attitudes toward decorum by citing the two parodies of it in Shakespeare. For it is surely clear that decorum is a term that is as unstable as it is often-cited. To cite the principle of decorum as though it were a clear and distinct idea is I think patently an error. But we can identify its general configurations and arrive at a wary but useful working definition.

The major "shapes" of decorum are two. The first is a concept which demands from the parts of a work of art consistency with established traditional social forms: this is *decorum personae*, decorum of the three styles, and decorum of the "kinds". There is a great variety and range even within this face of decorum. It can be as constricting as Webbe or as broad as Jonson. The second shape is

---

[141]   *Ibid.*, p. 290.
[142]   *Ibid.*, p. 1063.

vaguer but more important. It is a shape that has been felt rather than identified by modern scholars. This is the concept of the highest organic unity: decorum as at once the tool and ideal for adjusting proportions, relationships, colors to achieve a radiant whole. This is the Platonic and Aristotelian ideal. This is the Erasmian and Morean ideal, "the line & levell for al good makers to do their busines by". This is the idea which modern literary historians point at without defining in the best classical criticism. It is finally the decorum which Milton has in mind when he fights toward personal and aesthetic unity.

In attempting to identify this larger decorum I do not deny the smaller "rhetorical" one. Quite obviously the two co-exist, as has been shown, in Plato, Aristotle, and Erasmus. But without denying the more rigid and smaller uses of decorum, one can still suggest that the rhetorical and formal decorum, the decorum of the Rules, can sometimes act as a deterrent and diluter of the larger concept. This distortion or mis-emphasis we can see in some of the Alexandrian and medieval critics, in some of the Ciceronians, in Castelvetro, even in Sidney's one great *faux pas* in the *Apologie*.

It is possible and necessary to say that the concept of decorum is in its highest sense an ideal of unity as well as a tool of consistency, a vision of the highest unity – radiant, coherent and varied. This idea of decorum, it will be shown, is brilliantly developed and demonstrated in Milton. The roots of the Miltonic vision, the analogues and threats to it, are apparent in the tradition he inherited.[143]

---

[143]   Perhaps my feeling that Rosamund Tuve cites decorum as though it were too simply definable has prevented my using her monumental book, *Elizabethan and Metaphysical Imagery* (Chicago, 1947) as *the* point of departure. I have used consciously and unconsciously much of her scholarship and many of her insights. And if I feel some reservation about her definitions of decorum, I feel none in her use of the idea in her magnificent readings of "Comus" and "Lycidas" in *Images and Themes in Five Poems by Milton* (Cambridge, 1957).

Another important confrontation of the term decorum which I have not cited here is the unpublished dissertation of George Troxell Hemphill, "Decorum in English Verse ca. 1569-1700" (University of Minnesota, 1954). Because Mr. Hemphill considers the term strictly in relation to versification, our paths seldom cross.

II. DECORUM FROM THE PROSE

A. THE POET AS TRUE POEM

The seventeenth century critical term *decorum* had, as we have seen, considerable range. The firmness with which the term was cited does not necessarily mean that the term itself was stable or even absolutely clear in the instance. What was clear and firm was the need for decorum, its commanding position in the hierarchy of literary values. If it seems contradictory to insist on the primacy of a term which is not strictly defined, we have only to look at that other Renaissance term, *wit*,[1] or at modern terms like *imagination*.

Milton inherits a term which makes two kinds of demands on him. One face of decorum emphasises consistency, with emphasis on details of characterisation, style, and genre. This face of decorum Milton learned to respect at St. Paul's School[2] where the Latin exercises in prosopopoeiae emphasised rigid conformity to a pattern. The other face of decorum, the one which emphasised and urged unity and resonance, Milton would have learned from Plato and Aristotle or indeed from Puttenham. All the significant commentators on the term would have suggested to him that decorum, like wit, was a demanding but *Protean* term. In *The Arte of English Poesie* Milton could have found the two claims for the term on the same page.[3]

[1] For some of the problems involved in defining *wit*, see W. G. Crane, *Wit and Rhetoric in the Renaissance* (New York, 1937) and Arnold Stein, "Forms of Wit" in *Donne's Lyrics: The Eloquence of Action* (Minneapolis, 1962).

[2] Donald Lemen Clark, *John Milton at St. Paul's School: A Study of Ancient Rhetoric in English Renaissance Education* (New York, 1948), pp. 187-192, 206, 242-243, 244.

[3] See above, pp. 41-42

But of course Milton is not content to inherit; the parable of the talent is not casually present in his ambitions. The poet and prophet who aims at representing his people to history and to God is not likely to be satisfied with what he has received from the past he loves. The received idea of decorum is to be tested and enriched, submitted to the rigors of the great polemical ideas of the early part of the century. Milton's concept of decorum will be defined by him in the midst of struggle.

I should like to examine three groups of Milton's tracts in an attempt to find what he meant by decorum. The process of definition which operates here is complicated and difficult, but I think consistent. The result will not be a final stabilisation of the critical term and its being laid to rest in a glossary, but I hope that this examination will show that Milton was working through the claims of tradition and authority to determine what was "proper" in speech, in behavior, in life. I hope to show, too, that the rhetorical claims of decorum, of external consistency of detail, become for the great Puritan a minor, often a negative, aspect of the term.

I am not here describing how decorum works in the prose, though that is a part of my evidence; I am trying rather to see how Milton works at defining decorum. I am examining the prose for its comments on decorum, sometimes overt, sometimes by operation, sometimes through negatives. One starts by simply searching for the term and its synonyms, but the single word in Milton rarely represents the concept; it is necessary to submit oneself to the prose as a whole to see how the concept asserts itself.

I have chosen for examination the antiprelatical tracts, the divorce tracts and the three Defences. I have chosen these groups because they have a unity of subject matter within the group, and because the individual essay is likely to show slightly different pressures on the concept of decorum. I have chosen these groups also because they move chronologically and because they represent clear and rapid public expression. Allied to the rapidity and publicity of the essays is the reaction of contemporaries, who again and again accuse the grand master of decorum of indecorum. I have chosen these three groups finally because they assert themselves as commentators on decorum, when Milton defends his style from his attackers. Later, Milton himself makes this large claim for these prose works when he speaks of the "three species of liberty", which are essential to the happiness of social life – religious, domestic, and civil.[4]

The word *decorum* itself is in almost every case used in the limited rhetorical sense. Even in the claim for decorum as the "grand master peece" there is suggestion of radical superscription. But Milton suggests by his attack on other similar uses of the term and by his careful avoidance of the limited use in critical instances that there is a larger idea of propriety, of proper relation of surface and depth, than his opponents are summoning. The usual loci for Milton's use of decorum, the passages first collected by Ida Langdon in her pioneer study,[5] are, finally, inadequate to this larger idea which we see operating in Milton. If decorum seems a merely willful term for unity, I would point to the tradition of a larger decorum coexisting with a smaller, as I have shown above. I would point to the steady Miltonic attack on the minor face of decorum and the vacuum that attack creates. And finally I would point to the Miltonic habit of defining by opposites. Milton can use rhetorical decorum and even a little vainly. But his rhetorical decorum exists within a larger framework of philosophical and religious decorum. I shall try to trace that larger concept through the stresses and convergences of these prose works; then I should like to consider the conventional received statements on decorum and relate them to the larger context.

Milton's antiprelatical tracts have been often viewed as embarrassing mixtures of raptures and venom, rhetorically skilful but not finally worthy of the poet of *Paradise Lost*. In an attempt to represent these tracts more justly, the editors of volume one of the *Complete Prose Works* provide us with an enormous and valuable ap-

---

[4]   *The Works of John Milton*, ed. by Frank Allen Patterson *et al.*, 18 vols. (New York, 1931-1938), VIII, 131. Hereafter cited as Columbia *Milton* with volume and page number.

[5]   Ida Langdon, *Milton's Theory of Poetry and Fine Art* (New Haven, 1924), pp. 109-115, 232-35. For an application of Miss Langdon's findings see Kester Svendsen, "Epic Address and Reference and the Principle of Decorum in *Paradise Lost*", *Philological Quarterly*, XXVIII (Jan., 1949), 185-206.

paratus for the reconstruction of the context of this prose; and they include important suggestions on the way the language operates as an imaginative instrument for polemic. Occasionally however, there are lapses into apology for Milton's "masses of infamy, without discrimination",[6] and a kind of opposition is set up between the more or less temperate tenor of Bishop Hall's prose and the harshness of Milton's. In a note on that famous image of God vomiting over the bishops' deficiencies Don M. Wolfe and William Alfred write:

This image ... is a figure no one of Milton's Anglican opponents would have dared to use, even against the Puritans. For such a harsh metaphor Milton has tried to prepare his readers in the apologetic passage on "vehement Expressions".[7]

What is directly involved is Milton's decorum and our understanding of it, especially in comparison with Anglican decency.

I should like to argue that Milton's propriety is large enough and vital enough to comprehend and contain the passionate scurrility[8] which shocks us. I should like to argue, too, that Milton's propriety is an ideal of unity as well as a habit of adjusting the intensities of language to the situation. Often Milton's vision of unity is to be deduced from its opposite. Thus, the harmonious vision is to be inferred from the pejorative image of the diseased and deformed which masquerades as the flashy "outside". Kester Svendsen has argued this[9] and Don M. Wolfe and William Alfred themselves direct the reader toward remarking how "the governing image of the pamphlet, that of the members of the true church as members of the mystical body of Christ" is related to the metaphors for Episcopacy "of nausea, disease, and deformity".[10] Anglican decency, its cere-

---

[6] *Complete Prose Works of John Milton*, ed. by several hands (New Haven, 1953-), I, p. 536, note 72. Hereafter cited as Yale *Prose* with volume and page number.

[7] Yale *Prose*, I, p. 537, note 73.

[8] But I would like to remember W. R. Parker's Admonition, "Scurrility is scurrility, even if it is conventional, even if it is seemingly justified". *Milton's Contemporary Reputation* (Columbus, 1940), p. iii.

[9] *Milton and Science* (Cambridge, 1956), pp. 186-187, 191-192. Professor Svendsen's treatment of the antiprelatical tracts and the *Doctrine and Discipline of Divorce* seems to me to be brilliantly aware of the claims of the prose as prose.

[10] Yale *Prose*, I, 519,n.

monious wardrobe and language, is the object of Milton's furious attack. It becomes, too, a kind of inverse mirror which illuminates in a classic Miltonic procedure, "knowing good by evil", Milton's idea of radiant unity. I shall call this idea of unity, and the strategy of subordinating and relating local texture to that unity, *decorum*.

The propriety of Milton's prose is a fiery equilibrium of classic and neo-classic precepts, Christian traditions of language, and Miltonic aspirations, all tested in the religious controversies of the day. That propriety is no dead formula of received rhetorical precepts, nor is it something to be easily invoked for the testing of a given piece of discourse. The rules of the game are at least partly being written and revised as the game is played. I do not think this argues merely the fact of Milton's egoism, since that game is being played within a large and stable context which Milton never denies, his faith in God. So Milton's propriety of language is flexible and dynamic but Milton's propriety is not finally relativistic. The ends of discourse are the glorification of God, to repair the ruin of our first parents, to offer a lively sacrifice to God. All language bends and stretches to that purpose even when one of the delights of craftmanship is the delight of difficult conformity.

One of the most pervasive themes, or rather cluster of themes, in the antiprelatical tracts, is that of excess in language, frumpery, misused tradition, gaudiness. Milton again and again attacks the prelatical party for its excesses in language, clothing, and ritual. Indeed a great deal of the vigor in these tracts is to be found in the violence, contempt, and rough humor in his images of excess. The attack on excess, and occasionally on defect, is basically an attack on disharmony and disproportion, on the disparity or mis-relation of *inner* and *outer*, in the body, and the total man, and in the church and its rituals. Another way of expressing this is, quite simply, the separation of manner and matter, of letter and spirit.

Milton attacks the vestments of the Church, sometimes the real garments of Episcopacy, sometimes the garments as a metaphor for the exterior life of the church. At the beginning of *Of Reformation*, Milton refers to "the Jewish beggery, of old cast rudiments ... the new-vomited Paganisme of sensuall Idolatry".[11] He contrasts

[11] *Ibid.*, 520.

the "robes of pure innocency" with those "of pure Linnen, with other deformed, and fantastick dresses in Palls, and Miters, gold, and guegaw's fetcht from *Arons* old wardrope, or the *Flamins vestry*".[12]

This theme of garishness in clothing is related to the theme of excess in language.[13] Milton refuses to "run into a paroxysm of citations";[14] he denounces the "knotty Africanisms, the pamper'd metafors; the intricat, and involv'd sentences of the Fathers; besides the fantastick, and declamatory flashes; the crosse-jingling periods which cannot but disturb, and come thwart a setl'd devotion worse then the din of bells, and rattles".[15] Milton attacks those who call for Antiquity because "they feare the plain field of the Scriptures, the chase is too hot; they seek the dark, the bushie, the tangled Forrest, they would imbosk..."[16]

Of Prelatical Episcopacy continues with this imagery of excess in language and dress. Since the piece sets out to challenge the fathers,[17] there is more nearly total concern with "the broken reed of *tradition*";[18] Milton mocks "that indigested heap, and frie of Authors, which they call Antiquity".[19] In one high-colored passage he skilfully combines the images of clothing, nourishment, language and tradition:

---

[12] *Ibid.*, p. 521. Note also the contempt for the "Py-bald frippery" (*Ibid.*, p. 522) of the Prelates, who "overlai'd [the Gospel] with wanton *tresses*, and in a flaring tire bespecckl'd her with all the gaudy allurements of a Whore" (*Ibid.* p. 557). See also p. 612 for a list of absurd garments.

[13] This is a common theme in the Prolusions where it is not only related to Milton's hatred of Scholasticism, but has a life of its own and close connections with the problem of Milton's decorum, especially his rejection of 'mere' rhetorical propriety. See especially *Prolusions* I, III, and VI, and VII and the following pages in Yale *Prose* I, pp. 220, 239, 245, 271, 276, 300.

[14] Yale *Prose* I, 566.

[15] *Ibid.*, p. 568.

[16] *Ibid.*, p. 569. Again as in the *Prolusions* (Yale *Prose* I, pp. 211-306, *passim*) Milton's disdain for excess in language is mingled with contempt for pedantry in general. In Book II of *Of Reformation*, he speaks of the "art of policie" as "slubber'd with aphorisming pedantry" (*Ibid.*, I, 571), "*Rotchet Apothegmes*" and "*Pedantick palmes*" (*Ibid.*, p. 587).

[17] *Ibid.*, p. 620.

[18] *Ibid.*, p. 624.

[19] *Ibid.*, p. 626. On the following page, Milton speaks of "this vaine forraging", "these gay testimonies".

we doe injuriously in thinking to tast better the pure Euangelick Manna by seasoning our mouths with the tainted scraps, and fragments of an unknown table; and searching among the verminous, and polluted rags dropt overworn from the toyling shoulders of Time, with these deformedly to quilt, and interlace the intire, the spotlesse, and undecaying robe of Truth.[20]

In *Animadversions upon the Remonstrants Defence against Smectymnuus*, Milton again organizes his vituperation around the same images of excess. This time he is very much aware of the roughness of his prose. Just as he had defended his use of vehement expressions in the *Of Reformation*, he now defends himself in the preface to *Animadversions*:

And although in the serious uncasing of a grand imposture ... there be mixt here and there such a grim laughter, as may appeare at the same time in an austere visage, it cannot be taxt of levity or insolence: for even this veine of laughing (as I could produce out of grave Authors) hath ofttimes a strong and sinewy force in teaching and confuting...[21]

The whole preface is immediately relevant. Here is a defence of the grim laughter in terms of the concept of decorum – appropriateness to place, time, person, and especially subject – but one which scrupulously avoids mention of the many classical antecedents. It is easy to see this as purely a matter of strategy – i.e. the refusal to use authority because the opponent falls back on it. But Milton has not tried to suppress the question of decorum; he has insisted on making it completely overt. In a very real sense the question of decorum in the performance of religious duties and in the teaching of religion becomes *the* theme. The definition of the proper harmony between inner and outer, form and content, appearance and reality, becomes the major consideration. Milton could have cited Aristotle, Horace, Demetrius, even Scaliger in defence of his roughness. But he does not; he cites instead Solomon and Christ. And this is in keeping with the pervasive imagery of the total harmony of the inner and the outer man, and the attack on disharmony, excess, imbalance of the inner and outer man.

The last two antiprelatical tracts differ sharply in tone, the one is stately, the other sardonic. But both *The Reason of Church-gov-*

20   *Ibid.*, p. 639.
21   *Ibid.*, pp. 663-664.

ernment Urg'd Against Prelaty and *An Apology Against a Pamphlet*
contain the same basic referents in imagery; his "contempt for learned grubbing" implies "his love for true learning";[22] his contempt
for the externally garish and excessive implies his love for the har-
monies of inner and outer. Against "libidinous and ignorant Poetasters"[23] and the "Carnall textman"[24] he sets up the "interpreter
& relater of the best and sagest things".[25] After Milton confides
his plans for the future, he mentions with "what small willingnesse"
he left his "pleasing solitarynes" to come into "the dim reflexion
of hollow antiquities sold by the seeming bulk, and there be fain to
club quotations with men whose learning and beleif lies in marginal
stuffings".[26]

If, in *An Apology for Smectymnuus*, the rhythm of abuse quickens,
the theme is the same:

> For be not deceav'd, Readers, by men that would overawe your eares
> with big names and huge Tomes that contradict and repeal one another,
> because they can cramme a margent with citations. Do but winnow their
> chaffe from their wheat, ye shall see their great heape shrink and wax thin
> past beliefe.[27]

The point about the abundance of the imagery of excess in language,
dress, and "authority" is I think clear. And I have by no means ex-
hausted the examples. The antiprelatical tracts are full of them.
Often they are brilliantly fused with images of bodily illness. These
images of illness are startling and have already received attention,[28]
but I should like to reexamine them, to show they are related to the
images discussed above, and to suggest that Milton has organized
his tracts around the master image of excess and disharmony; only
if we recognize this master image can we grasp the remarkable co-
herence, the true decorum of this prose.

First, Milton himself demonstrates how functionally right his ill-

---

[22]   The phrases are those of Ralph A. Haug, editor of *The Reason of Church-
government*, in Yale *Prose*, I, 737.
[23]   *Ibid.*, p. 818.
[24]   *Ibid.*, p. 951.
[25]   *Ibid.*, p. 811. For further Miltonic examples of Episcopal speciousness and
excess see pp. 765, 779, 792.
[26]   *Ibid.*, pp. 821-822.
[27]   *Ibid.*, p. 945. See also pp. 872, 873, 910, 920, 922, 935.
[28]   Svendsen, *Milton and Science*, pp. 174-210.

ness image is in this clearly articulated metaphor of bodily excess
with spiritual want:

> for in very deed, the superstitious man by his good will is an Atheist; but
> being scarr'd from thence by the pangs, and gripes of a boyling con-
> science, all in a pudder shuffles up to himselfe such a *God*, and such a
> *worship* as is most agreeable to remedy his feare, which feare of his, as
> also is his hope, fixt onely upon the *Flesh*, renders likewise the whole
> faculty of his apprehension, carnall, and all the inward acts of *worship*
> issuing from the native strength of the SOULE, run out lavishly to the
> upper skin, and there harden into a crust of Formallitie.[29]

This example is characteristic, demonstrating as it does a literally
fluid, dynamic relationship of the inner body (and by extension,
soul) and the outer; unpleasantly, but consequently, Milton's most
effective images of bodily disarrangement are done in terms of tu-
mors and excrescences[30] and regurgitation.

If these disarrangements strike us as shocking, we must remember
that they are derived from the traditional use of the body as metaphor for order. "Diseased flesh and blood", Professor Svendsen
writes, "imply always the opposite: the possibility of order in men
and institutions".[31] When the ideal of harmony and order is so often cited as an end, we must accept as relevant the idea of disorder. Again we must remember Milton's injunction on knowing
good by knowing evil, and we must point, with Professor Svendsen,
to the ease, consistency, and appropriateness of the images of bodily
disorder in the prose.[32] As one examines the imagery of the prose,
he becomes more and more aware of the obsessive image of unity
in Milton. It is shown again and again in the way he relates inner to
outer, in the way the outer portrays the inner, and the way the inner
flows out to the outer. A study of the prose of Milton becomes in
large part a study of the way things are complexly unified or related,
and the dangerous ways in which they are disunified. The images
of unity show fluid and complex ways of unity; the images of disunity show fluid and complex disarrangements. Internal corruption or disarrangement flows out into external sores or vomit; but

[29]   Yale *Prose*, I, 522.
[30]   See for example the Fable of the Wen, *Ibid.*, p. 584.
[31]   Svendsen, *Milton and Science*, p. 193.
[32]   *Ibid.*, p. 186.

even more horrifying is the cosmetic exterior, the attempt to beautify the outside without the prerogative of interior sanctity. The inward truth is sufficient unto itself: "he that will cloath the Gospel now, intimates plainly, that the Gospel is naked, uncomely..."[33] The cosmetician is wrong about scripture when he attempts to beautify it, he is misestimating scripture when he tries to "cover and hide his righteous verity with the polluted cloathing of your ceremonies to make it seem more decent in your own eyes".[34]

The inward truth is sufficient unto itself; it does not need cosmetic. But that does not imply, and the point is important, that it lacks its own glow or its proper outside. The rejection of false emphasis and misproportion does not mean the rejection of the physical. Occasionally it will mean that one aspect of the physical takes precedence over another. The human body is never denied by Milton; it is given enormous value when it is purely or properly related to the life of the spirit.

[the good Christian] will stirre him up to walk worthy the honourable and grave imployment wherewith God and the Church hath dignifi'd him: not fearing lest he should meet with some outward holy thing in religion which his lay touch or presence might profane, but lest something unholy from within his own heart should dishonour and profane in himselfe that Priestly unction and Clergy-right whereto Christ hath entitl'd him.[35]

The reference here is quite clearly to the Canons of 1640, and especially to the hated rail before the Communion Table:

And because experience hath shewed us, how irreverent the behaviour of people is in many places ... it is thought meet and convenient by this present Synod, that the said Communion Tables in all Chancells or Chappells, be decently severed with Rails to preserve them from such or worse profanations.[36]

The decency which the bishops here call for is an important consideration in the reading of Milton's early prose. The whole perspective of these tracts depends on the recognition that Anglican

---

[33] Yale *Prose*, I, 828.
[34] *Ibid.*
[35] *Ibid.*, p. 844.
[36] "Constitutions and Canons Ecclesiastical", in Yale *Prose*, I, 992. See also "The London Petition" (1640), Yale *Prose*, I, 976-984, esp. 980-981, for Puritan response to the Canons.

decency for Milton represents a concentration on the spurious exterior of things; decorum, the proper balance of inner and outer, is partly to be glimpsed in the visions of the future, partly to be deduced from the negative images of prelatical excess. The image of the diseased and garrulous traditionalist is to be countered with the vision of the healthy, radiant, singing body.

For Puttenham, decency and decorum were synonyms. But by 1616, Thomas Wilson's *A Christian Dictionary* suggests that the term was being commandeered by the Anglicans to represent traditional ceremoniousness, the proper ritual dignity in church service, vestments and furnishings. That which is decent, Wilson writes "of its owne nature brings some dignity and comelinesse to divine actions, as a Table and a Table-cloth at the Communion, a Pulpit, and a Pulpit-cloth to a Sermon".[37] Wilson ends by citing the standard text in defence of decency, as does Bishop Hall in his *Holy Decency in the Worship of God*:

It is a thing well-pleasing to God, that there should be all outward cleanliness, gravity, reverent and comely postures, meet furniture, utensils, places, used and observed in the service of the Almighty: a truth sufficiently grounded upon that irrefragable canon of the Apostle, *Let all things be done decently, and in order* (I Cor. xiv, 40); whereof *order* refers to persons and actions; *decency* to the things done and the fashion of doing them.[38]

Hall is not naive about the term; he recognizes its relativism,[39] but turns to "Right Reason, Undebauched Nature, and approved Custom",[40] rules for the regulation and judgment of decency.

Hall's defence recognizes the primacy of inner worship, but he is more concerned to establish the necessity for exterior comeliness. The proper balance between inner and outer, the "holy reverence"[41]

[37] Thomas Wilson, *A Christian Dictionary* (London, 1616), p. 118.
[38] *Works*, ed. by Peter Hall (London, 1837), VI, 464.
[39] I can not do justice here to the related and very important question of "Indifferency". It is a critical and burning issue to Robert Greville, Lord Brooke, *A Discourse opening the Nature of that Episcopacie, which is exercised in England, 1641*, printed in *Tracts on Liberty in the Puritan Revolution*, ed. by William Haller (New York, 1933), II; and Milton speaks of "a needlesse and jolly persecuter call'd Indifference", Yale *Prose* I, 925.
[40] *Works*, VI, 465.
[41] *Ibid.*, p. 473.

of decency, is to be found in the Church of England, the *via media* between Rome's "unjust excess"[42] and Geneva's "nasty carelessness".[43] The demands of the controversy of course move Hall to emphasize the exaggerations of Puritan attitude:

> clay and sticks please them better than marble and cedar ... the very dogs are allowed free access and leave to lift up their legs at those Holy Tables, where we partake of the Son of God.[44]

Hall's freedom of language here is independently interesting; and the relation of Hall to Milton is enough to make us interested in his comments. But perhaps the most influential Anglican statement on decency is Archbishop Laud's. In the 1639 edition of *A Relation of the Conference between ... Laud ... and Mr. Fisher the Jesuite*, the unfortunate prelate addressed the king on the matter:

> No One thing hath made Conscientious men more wavering in their owne mindes, or more apt, and easie to be drawne aside from the sincerity of Religion professed in the Church of England, then the Want of Uniforme and Decent Order in too many Churches of the Kingdome ... Tis true, the Inward Worship of the Heart, is the Great Service of God, and no Service acceptable without it: But the Externall worship of God in his Church is the Great Witness to the World, that Our heart stands right in that Service of God ... These thoughts are they, and no other, which have made me labour so much, as I have done, for Decency and an orderly settlement of the Externall Worship of God in the Church. For of that which is Inward there can be no Witnesse among men, nor no Example for men. Now no Externall Action in the world can be Uniforme without some Ceremonies. And these in Religion, the Ancienter they bee, the better, so they may fit Time and Place... Ceremonies are the Hedge that fence the Substance of Religion from all the Indignities, which Prophanesse and Sacriledge too Commonly put upon it.[45]

---

[42] *Ibid.*, p. 467. See also "Epistles Decade V" in Hall's *Works*, VI, 242.

[43] Hall, *Works*, VI, 464.

[44] *Ibid.*

[45] William Laud, *A Relation of the Conference between ... Laud ... and Mr. Fisher the Jesuit ...* (London, 1639), sig. *3. See also Laud's *A Speech Delivered in the Starr-Chamber ... Concerning pretended Innovations In the Church* (London, 1637), pp. 46-47 and *passim*. George Herbert uses the term *decency* in this same sense of Anglican ritual propriety, but in the sweet and simple context of *The Country Parson*, decency could scarcely offend even Milton; see *The Works of George Herbert*, ed. by F. E. Hutchinson (Oxford, 1953), p. 246.

The Puritan attack on Laud is a central episode in the conflict of King and Parliament and a good part of Puritan polemics is devoted to the attack on Laudian decency or aspects of it. The controversial literature is full of debates over the placement and the name of the Altar, bowing at the name of Jesus, the use of music, vestments, Church ornaments. The bibliography on Anglican decency and its decline and fall would be enormous, as the Catalogue of the Thomason Collection and the Short Title Catalogues suggest;[46] one can view Prynne's enormous *Canterburies Doome* as itself a catalogue of the sins of Laudian decency. Therefore, it is impossible here to do full justice to the question. One can only point to several signs of the importance of the idea and then relate it to Milton.

In *Lords Bishops* (1640), Prynne makes scornful reference to Laud's words to the king:

And indeed such *Ceremonies hedge in and fence his Romish Religion*, while in the meane time they *hedge* out the *true Religion* ... no *Decency*, no *Orderly Settlement*. But by his leave, he must not call this the *worship of God*. For *God* abhorres all such *will-worship* as a *vaine worship*, and meere *hipocricy*, and the fruite and signe of a prowd, carnall, profane, and unbeleeving heart.[47]

Another answer to Laud and one which shows the same vehement reversal of Anglican attitude is Henry Burton's *A Replie to a Relation of the Conference Betweene William Laude and Mr. Fisher the Jesuite*:

But what doe you call *Decencie?* Certainly that onely is *Decent* in the *worship* of *God*, which *God* himselfe approveth, and that is onely That, which himselfe *commandeth* in his *word*. But you account and call that onely *Decent* in the *worship* of *God*, which your selfe, or that Whore of *Babylon* hath devised for *Decent*, as the seting up of her pompous *Devotion* and *voluntary humility* in Rites and Ceremonies in *Gods worship*, as ye pretend... Will Christ (trow you) aporove [approve] that for *decent* in his *Spouse*, which is the *Whores* Fashion?[48]

[46] See the convenient brief bibliography in Will T. Hale's edition of *Of Reformation* (New Haven and London, 1916), p. 83, and the bibliography in Yale *Prose*, I, 526 n.
[47] William Prynne, *Lords Bishops* (London, 1640), sig. G3-G3ᵛ.
[48] (London, 1640), p. 83. The symbolic garishness of Rome and the slovenliness of Geneva which Donne shows us is in the "Satyre III" and Herbert in "The British Church" are steadily used by Anglican controversialists. The Puritans, of course, tend to describe Rome more, and Geneva less, extremely.

But what is most interesting and relevant is decency's burning importance for Milton, who takes the argument over the fit expression of the internal and puts it at the heart of his arguments on the government of church, state, and individual. Perhaps in response to a certain vulnerability and querulousness, at the least defensiveness, in Anglican apologetics, he attacks the claims for the *via media*, imposing stricter and more comprehensive ideas of unity and purity than other writers. Milton insists that "decency" is an imbalance with excess of external worship and defects of internal purity.[49]

The argument against decency is present in all of Milton's antiprelatical writings. Even the early "A Postscript", which he wrote for the Smectymnuans, claims that Anglicanism has tried "to hinder all further reformation" by increasing ceremonies and turning "all Religion into a pompous outside".[50] In the magnificent opening paragraph of *Of Reformation*, Milton had attacked the Prelates for

cloaking their Servile crouching to all *Religious* Presentments, somtimes lawfull, sometimes Idolatrous, under the name of *humility*, and terming the Py-bald frippery, and ostentation of Ceremony's, decency.[51]

With bitter intensity, Milton describes the barriers which decency erects between man and his religion; the passage is like a prophecy of tracts to come:

the Table of Communion now become a Table of separation stands like an exalted platforme upon the brow of the quire, fortifi'd with bulwark, and barricado, to keep off the profane touch of the Laicks, whilst the obscene, and surfeted Priest scruples not to paw, and mammock the sacramentall bread, as familiarly as his Tavern Bisket. And thus the peopled vilifi'd and rejected by them...[52]

---

[49] The importance of the issue is argued persuasively, and with very different conclusions, by E. C. E. Bourne, *The Anglicanism of William Laud* (London, 1947). Reverend Bourne gives an extreme Anglican reading of Puritan attitudes toward decency. He finds Puritanism "more Manichaean than Christian" (p. 38). Milton is cited as an arrogant exception to the Puritan effort to "mortify the deeds of the flesh" (p. 39) but the overwhelming impression of the first part of the book is that the Puritans willfully misinterpreted decency. Reverend Bourne oversimplifies, I think; I cite him here as witness to the centrality of the controversy over decency.

[50] Yale *Prose*, I, 975. For the argument for Milton's authorship of the *Postscript*, see Yale *Prose*, I, 960-964.

[51] *Ibid.*, p. 522.

[52] *Ibid.*, p. 547-548.

Separation, disparity, pretentiousness and impurity in the religious experience become compulsive concerns of Milton in this prose. Milton speaks of "your inside nakednesse"[53] and scorns "your Priest under the Gospell that thinks himselfe the purer, or the cleanlier in his office for his new washt Surplesse".[54] Referring to *Isaiah*, he writes:

Are the feet so beautifull, and is the very bringing of these tidings so decent of it self? what new decency then can be added to this by your spinstry? ye think by these gaudy glisterings to stirre up the devotion of the rude multitude; ye think so, because ye forsake the heavenly teaching of S. *Paul* for the hellish Sophistry of Papism.[55]

In the concern about decency are implicit the major concerns of Milton's prose and poetry, the demands for discipline and freedom, Christian liberty, temperance, and the language of inspiration. The Anglican claims for proportion in decency arouse more rigorous demands in Milton, even where the initial claim is for simplicity:

For that which the Apostles taught hath freed us in religion from the *ordinances of men*, and commands that *burdens be not laid* upon the redeemed of Christ, though the formalist will say, what no decency in Gods worship? Certainly Readers, the worship of God singly in it selfe, the very act of prayer and thanksgiving with those free and unimpos'd expressions which from a sincere heart unbidden come into the outward gesture, is the greatest decency that can be imagin'd.[56]

The violent imagery of these tracts is channeled toward the destruction of Anglican decency in all its misproportion. The pressure behind the waves of excoriation is the concept of decorum, Milton's well-proportioned unity, the radiant harmony, the harmonious vision.[57] This unity had already been projected by Milton in the "Nativity Ode" in "Comus" and even in his *Prolusions*; we are to

---

[53] *Ibid.*, p. 668.

[54] *Ibid.*, p. 728-729.

[55] *Ibid.*, p. 828. See also the attack on the universities for sending home men "with such a scholastical burre in their throats, as hath stopt and hinderd all true and generous philosophy from entring, crackt their voices for ever with metaphysical gargarisms, and hath made them admire a sort of formal outside men prelatically addicted ... " (*Ibid.*, p. 854).

[56] *Ibid.*, pp. 941-2.

[57] My use of this phrase without quotation marks should suggest the pervasive influence of Don Cameron Allen's *The Harmonious Vision* (Baltimore, 1954).

see its continual development and exemplification in the prose to follow and in the great poems. Always it exists with its antitype, flawed proportion, disunity, speciousness.

We are here more aware of the disunity than the unity; and with many modern critics,[58] there stand a good number of Milton's contemporaries who find too difficult the fierce equation of Miltonic decorum. Milton had "authority" for his broad conception of decorum, as I have tried to show. But he does not cite authority;[59] he builds his propriety from the inside rather than applying it from the outside, and he pays the price in losing the understanding and sympathy of many of his readers. Thomas Fuller, for example, accuses Milton of a violation of decorum in the *Of Reformation*:

And one lately hath traduced them [the bishops] with such language as neither beseemed his parts whosoever he was that spake it, nor their piety of whom it was spoken.[60]

The reason for the critical miscalculation here, and elsewhere in criticism of the prose, is the failure to see that Milton's various streams of abuse are united under the theme of excess or disharmony and that this master theme of itself asserts the existence of its opposite: order, harmony, decorum.

We are dealing with two contexts which oppose each other and yet use each other for definition. Decency is a conception of elegant moderation to Bishop Hall, of nauseating lukewarmness to Milton.

[58] See Hale *op. cit.* p. xlvi: "we are conscious that only one whose beautiful soul had a moral taint could have uttered ... so dire a curse ..." Elsewhere Hale speaks of Puritan (and presumably Miltonic) hatred of beauty, "fondness for the uncouth", short-sightedness. See pp. xxviii, xxix, xxx, xlvi and *passim*. This is the edition which the Yale editors call "a model of scholarly precision and imagination". See Don M. Wolfe and William Alfred, "Preface" to *Of Reformation*, in Yale *Prose*, I, 515. One senses something like hostility to Milton's strategy in the antiprelatical tracts in some of the notes to this latest edition. See p. 520 n. 4, p. 529 n. 45, p. 554 n. 128. Even Arthur E. Barker, in his brilliant treatment of the prose, suggests that "the residuum of positive thinking in the antiprelatical tracts is seen to be remarkably small". *Milton and the Puritan Dilemma* (Toronto, 1942), p. 21.

[59] He does not even cite John Calvin on decorum. See *Institutes of the Christian Religion*, trans. by John Allen, 2 vols. (Philadelphia, n.d.), II, 478. We might remember, in passing, Milton's "as if we could be put off with *Calvins* name, unlesse we be convinc't with *Calvins* reason" (Yale *Prose*, I, 707).

[60] Quoted in Hale's edition of *Of Reformation*, p. xxxv. Cf. Yale *Prose*, I, 532 n.

Zeal is the foundation of religious attitude and language for Milton, for Archbishop Laud it is the enemy of church-government. We can mention a whole series of words which affect the two parties in almost diametrically opposite ways. Zeal, enthusiasm, decency, ceremony – no single definition of any of these terms would represent the age. The parallel lines never meet. In the matter of religious attitude, we might even set up opposing biblical texts for the strategy of the two parties. The Anglicans often cite from I Corinthians, *Let all things be done decently and in order*; the Puritans use Revelation 3:16, *So then because thou art lukewarm, and neither cold nor hot, I will spew thee out of my mouth*. Both texts summon long and rich traditions.[61] Herbert comes immediately to mind as a native of Anglican decency, while the Puritan tradition of religious zeal and opposition to lukewarmness is at its peak in Milton.

The distinctions of attitude, one could say of decorum, extend toward language. In the Smectymnuan controversy, for example, each party comments at length on the way the other side misuses language. It is not only that there is so much talk about language, but that the same discourse can seem to one group *"passionate Rhetorications"*[62] and to another "so meek and gallesse a Discourse".[63] The problem of language is a constant concern of the controversialists as Milton's steady attack on Anglican excesses would suggest. The Anglican attack on the rhetoric of zeal is just as steady. Bishop Hall calls for moderation in language again and again, as in the eleventh rule from *Christian Moderation* (1640), "To refrayne from all rayling termes, and spightfull provocations in differences of Religion".[64] In his "Speech to Starr-Chamber" (1637) Archbishop Laud is bitter about "these *Libellers, mouthes* and *pennes*…"[65] Richard Hooker asks, "Who seeth not how full gorged they are with virulent, slanderous, and immodest speeches,

---

[61] I have studied the tradition of Puritan commentary on this verse of Revelation in "Milton and the Rhetoric of Zeal", *Texas Studies in Literature and Language*, Winter, 1965.

[62] This is the accusation laid against Bishop Hall by the Smectymnuans. See *An Answer to a Book Entituled An Humble Remonstrance* (London, 1641), p. 2.

[63] This phrase, in Hall's defence, is in *A Defence of the Humble Remonstrance Against the frivolous and false exceptions of Smectymnuus* (London, 1641), p. 1.

[64] (London, 1640), p. 151.

[65] (London, 1637), p. 73.

tending much to the disgrace, to the disproofe nothing of that cause, which they endeavour to overthrow?"[66]

Milton's interest in language is not unusual for his time, nor even for his party, though it may be unique in its intensity and breadth. He attacks Anglican speciousness in language whether for ornateness or for pretentious simplicity.[67] But he is not averse to stressing the surface conformities when they are useful. This is especially true in the last of the antiprelatical tracts *An Apology Against A Pamphlet...*, where Milton answers and enters a number of quibbles on his style and that of his opponent,[68] the anonymous author of *A Modest Confutation of a Slanderous and Scurrilous Libell, Entituled, Animadversions, etc.* The modest confuter had attacked Milton's style, learning and character and had shown special indignation at Milton's defence according to the precepts of Solomon and Christ:

> *Horrid blasphemy*! You *that love Christ and know this miscreant wretch,* stone *him to death, least yourselves smart for his impunity.*[69]

Although Milton responds with some strictly technical comments on satire[70] and on decorum of reference,[71] basically he depends on the same kind of argument he had summoned earlier. There are signs of weariness or disappointment[72] at the rejection of his preface to *Animadversions*, but the claim to propriety is still firmly Christian. The by-passing of classical authority is deliberate:

---

[66]   *Certain Briefe Treatises, Written by Diverse Learned Men, concerning the ancient and Moderne government of the Church* (Oxford, 1641), p. 4.
[67]   See the attack on Hall's "spruce fastidious oratory" (Yale *Prose*, I, 670). In *An Apology Against a Pamphlet*, Milton wrote: "I took it as my part the lesse to endure that my respected friends ... should thus lye at the mercy of a coy flurting stile; to be girded with frumps and curtall gibes, by one who makes sentences by the Statute, as if all above three inches long were confiscat" (Yale *Prose*, I, 872-873).
[68]   One can find this increasing emphasis in the Divorce tracts and the *Defences* also. In these groups, too, the last tract is the most defensive on rhetorical grounds. See the *Colasterion* and the *Pro Se Defensio*.
[69]   Parker, *Milton's Contemporary Reputation*, p. iii.
[70]   Yale *Prose*, I, 916. See 914-915 for further discussion of this genre. And see 934 for Milton's comments on the kinds of style.
[71]   *Ibid.*, p. 920.
[72]   *Ibid.*, p. 871.

If therefore the question were in oratory, whether a vehement vein throwing out indignation, or scorn upon an object that merits it, were among the aptest *Ideas* of speech to be allow'd, it were my work, and that an easie one to make it cleare both by the rules of best rhetoricians, and the famousest examples of Greek and Roman Orations. But since the Religion of it is disputed, and not the art, I shall make use only of such reasons and autorities, as religion cannot except against.[73]

We must note that though the antiprelatical tracts do not summon "the rules of best rhetoricians", there is an implication that these rules have a parallel, as it were substantiating, life. Only rarely does Milton suggest that the religious view clashes with the classical rhetorical view. There is rather the assumption that Christian decorum contains classical, rhetorical decorum. So, Milton's defence of "the vehement vein" is not from Demetrius, but from Christ:

Our Saviour ... was Lord to expresse his indoctrinating power in what sort him best seem'd; sometimes by a milde and familiar converse, sometimes with plaine and impartiall home-speaking regardlesse of those whom the auditors might think he should have had in more respect; otherwhiles with bitter and irefull rebukes if not teaching yet leaving excuselesse those his wilfull impugners. What was all in him, was divided among many others the teachers of his Church; some to be severe and ever of a sad gravity that they may win such, & check sometimes those who be of nature over-confident and jocond; others were sent more cheerefull, free, and still as it were at large, in the midst of an untrespassing honesty; that they who are so temper'd may have by whom they might be drawne to salvation, and they who are too scrupulous, and dejected of spirit might be often strengthn'd with wise consolations and revivings: no man being forc't wholly to dissolve that groundwork of nature which God created in him, the sanguine to empty out all his sociable livelinesse, the cholerick to expell quite the unsinning predominance of his anger; but that each radicall humour and passion wrought upon and corrected as it ought, might be made the proper mould and foundation of every mans peculiar guifts, and vertues.[74]

This is consistent with classical theory of discourse designed πρὸς τὸν ἀκροατήν: this "regard to the audience" is consistent with Colet's theory of accommodation; and it is consistent with Milton's own practice in the prose.

---

[73] *Ibid.*, p. 899.
[74] *Ibid.*, pp. 899-900.

In speaking of Christ's own freedom of language, Milton goes farther than the modest confuters of his time:

is it blasphemy, or any whit disagreeing from Christian meeknesse, when as Christ himselfe speaking of unsavory traditions, scruples not to name the Dunghill and the Jakes, for me to answer a slovenly wincer...[75] Doth not Christ himselfe teach the highest things by the similitude *of old bottles and patcht cloaths?* Doth he not illustrate best things by things most evill?...[76] Turne then to the first of Kings where God himselfe uses the phrase; *I will cut off from Iereboam him that pisseth against the wall.* Which had it beene an unseemely speech in the heat of an earnest expression, then we must conclude that *Ionathan, or Onkelos the Targumists* were of cleaner language then he that made the tongue... Whereas God who is the author both of purity and eloquence, chose this phrase as fittest in that vehement character wherein he spake... Fools who would teach men to read more decently then God thought good to write. And thus I take it to be manifest, that indignation against men and their actions notoriously bad, hath leave and autority oft times to utter such words and phrases as in common talke were not so mannerly to use.[77]

This is as far as Milton will go toward a "literary" defence.

What emerges from this study of the antiprelatical tracts is a pervading concept of harmony, radiant unity, *decorum* which takes life from, and gives life to, the rhetoric of disharmony, illness, excess. There emerges, too, Milton's refusal to mention the rhetorical issues in other than their religious applications. There emerges an insistence on freedom of style based upon the propriety of it in terms of the subject, the goal of the inquiry. Only in the *Apology* does Milton heavily reinforce this argument with literary examples from scripture and rhetorical rules based on these religious *occasions*. No where does Milton deny the beauty of language, its embellishment. Almost everywhere he insists on the suppleness, flexibility, and range of language. Everywhere he insists on the inner life of the word. Milton uses the word *carnall* freely and pejoratively. But his description of the healthy body, or language, or garment is rarely crabbed or ascetic.

Throughout the tracts we have had visions of the healthy body,

[75] *Ibid.*, p. 895.
[76] *Ibid.*, p. 898.
[77] *Ibid.*, pp. 902-3.

as individual, as state, as church. At the very opening of the first tract we have the Doctrine of the *Gospel*,

refin'd to such a Spirituall height, and temper of purity, and knowledge of the Creator, that the body, with all the circumstances of time and place, were purifi'd by the affections of the regenerat Soule, and nothing left impure, but sinne...[78]

Very richly in the *Reason of Church-government* we find a respect for the whole self:

And if the love of God ... be the first principle of all godly and vertuous actions in men, this pious and just honouring of our selves is the second, and may be thought as the radical moisture and fountain head, whence every laudable and worthy enterprize issues forth.[79]

But he that holds himself in reverence and due esteem, both for the dignity of Gods image upon him, and for the price of his redemption ... accounts himselfe both a fit person to do the noblest and godliest deeds, and much better worth then to deject and defile, with such a debasement and such a pollution as sin is, himselfe so highly ransom'd and enobl'd to a new friendship and filiall relation with God. Nor can he fear so much the offence and reproach of others, as he dreads and would blush at the reflection of his own severe and modest eye upon himselfe, if it should see him doing or imagining that which is sinfull though in the deepest secrecy. How shall a man know to do himselfe this right, how to performe this honourable duty of estimation and respect towards his own soul and body? which way will leade him best to this hill top of sanctity and goodnesse above which there is no higher ascent but to the love of God which from this self-pious regard cannot be assunder?[80]

The harmony of inner and outer man is not renunciation; it is proportion. Hence the rightness, not disparity, of his descriptions of the poems to come and the man who is to create them:

Then amidst the *Hymns*, and *Halleluiahs* of *Saints* some one may perhaps bee heard offering at high *strains* in new and lofty *Measures* to sing and celebrate thy *divine Mercies*, and *marvelous Judgements* in this Land throughout all AGES; whereby this great and Warlike Nation instructed and inur'd to the fervent and continuall practice of *Truth* and *Righteous-*

---

[78]   *Ibid.*, p. 519.
[79]   *Ibid.*, p. 841.
[80]   *Ibid.*, p. 842. In the same passage Milton attacks the decency of the Prelates who have "driven holinesse out of living into livelesse things", and for having "proclaim'd the best of creatures, mankind, so unpurifi'd and contagious ..." (*Ibid.*, pp. 844-845).

nesse, and casting farre from her the *rags* of her old *vices* may presse on hard to that *high* and *happy* emulation to be found the *soberest, wisest,* and *most Christian People*...[81]

This is the harmony we have insisted on. And though the word *sober* may bother some, there is nothing here of asceticism. There is richness, in the harmony, as resonance and complexity. The same effect is in the passage from *Animadversions*:

And he that now for haste snatches up a plain ungarnish't present as a thanke-offering to thee, which could not bee deferr'd in regard of thy so many late deliverances wrought for us one upon another, may then perhaps take up a Harp, and sing thee an elaborate Song to Generations.[82]

The imagery in these two passages operates in such a way that we tend to clothe *decorously* the singing figure. What we have then is the harmonious organic vision which gives meaning to, as it takes meaning from, a passage like this:

And it is still *Episcopacie* that before all our eyes worsens and sluggs the most learned, and seeming religious of our *Ministers*, who no sooner advanc't to it, but like a seething pot set to coole, sensibly exhale and reake out the greatest part of that zeale, and those Gifts which were formerly in them, settling in a skinny congealment of ease and sloth at the top: and if they keep their Learning by some potent sway of Nature, 'tis a rare chance; but their *devotion* most commonly comes to that queazy temper of luke — warmnesse, that gives a Vomit to GOD himselfe.[83]

The unity of the human body and soul, its language, clothing and traditions is both a complex vehicle for Milton's polemical opinions and a superior theme in the antiprelatical tracts. Milton argues his position using the tools of this larger decorum of unity, and finally it is this higher unity he is arguing *for*. In the famous passage on his early reading, Milton gives us a climactic personal vision of the kind of harmony he means, the ultimate fusion of inner and outer:

And long it was not after, when I was confirm'd in this opinion, that he who would not be frustrate of his hope to write well hereafter in laudable things, ought him selfe to bee a true Poem, that is, a composition, and

[81]   *Ibid.*, p. 616.
[82]   *Ibid.*, p. 706.
[83]   *Ibid.*, pp. 536-7. For a more detailed analysis of this image and its relation to biblical commentary and the rhetoric of zeal, see my "Milton and the Rhetoric of Zeal".

patterne of the best and honourablest things; not presuming to sing high praises of heroick men, or famous Cities, unlesse he have in himselfe the experience and the practice of all that which is praise-worthy.[84]

This is not some spectacular and interpolated naivete, but an intense working theme and program for the antiprelatical tracts.

B. OUR MANHOOD IN GRACE

The episode of Milton's marriage has been called by Professor Hanford "the *pons asinorum* of his biographers".[85] One feels that much of the twentieth century baiting of the poet uses this event to generalize on Milton's personality and then to impose those generalizations on his verse. So the clichés of Robert Graves' novel contribute to the working vocabulary for a critic like A. J. A. Waldock or John Peter.[86] The result is, I think, a kind of critical error which is indulging itself in talk about the failure of human relations or humanity in the great poems, after having failed to engage precisely the human relations and humanity of the prose. One can approach the divorce tracts in such a way as to read them only as corroborative material to the tradition of Milton's anti-feminism and egoism. I hope my reading does not succumb to this convenient single-sightedness.

I am seeking comments on decorum, but I am trying to read the prose as literature, trying to see it whole, so that my emphases will not be major distractions. I cannot do this wholly successfully, but my concern with the language of the tracts will, I hope, help me to avoid too personal direction.

We are faced with the problem of Milton's personality and reputation. We must allow that Milton's personality is a part of these tracts; if we had no record of Mary Powell, we would still feel the assertion of self in the one gentle stroking of this prose. The poet is here and here complexly. At the very least for Milton the poet is ✓ analogous to the poem: "ought him selfe to bee a true Poem". We

---

[84] Yale *Prose*, I, 890.
[85] James Holly Hanford, *John Milton, Englishman* (New York, 1949), p. 113.
[86] For discussion of the criticism of Professors Waldock and Peter, see below.

feel the writer urgently here but as writer and debater and public voice, rarely as disappointed husband.[87]

The disappointed husband is a figure taken from the Milton reputation and imposed, just so, on the divorce pamphlets; the urgency is thus translated to stridency, the mercy to self-pity, the heroic rationalism to egoism, and the confusion to hate. These negative emotions may be there but if so they are a minor part of the whole.

These five pamphlets are in many ways beautifully articulated with the rest of the work, and in many ways rigorously impersonal and public. At the same time, the impersonal and public aspects do not exclude mercy, sympathy, pity for the human condition. The brilliant visionary optimism about marriage does not obviate the necessity for tolerance of human weakness.

The divorce tracts are a group in subject and in time; all five (including the second and much expanded edition of the *Doctrine and Discipline of Divorce*) were published between August, 1643, and March, 1645.[88] The two editions of the *Doctrine and Discipline* and the *Tetrachordon* strike the reader as major works, with Milton deeply engaged. *The Judgment of Martin Bucer* and *Colasterion* are "incidental salvos", [89] but consistent and often intensive. The divorce tracts occupied Milton for two years of his maturity. They represent a major phase in his middle years.

I should like to argue that the divorce tracts are related to the antiprelatical tracts in their treatment of Decorum, which by now I quite frankly assume to mean the highest unity. The theme of wholeness, of radiant and unconstricted harmony, of the organically various unity is at, or very near, the heart of these tracts. Again, Milton defines through opposites, using some of the same imagery as in the antiprelatical tracts; again his range is extraordinary and his freedom too rich for the blood of his contemporaries; and again he moves to a narrower defence of self in the last tract.

---

[87] What Ann Davidson Ferry has done for the voice of the narrator in *Paradise Lost*, in *Milton's Epic Voice* (Cambridge, 1963), ought to be done, for critical passages at least, in the prose. I do not wholly agree with Miss Ferry in some of her descriptions of the distance between the speaker and John Milton, but the method I find useful and the isolation of the problem important.

[88] Yale *Prose*, II, 217, 719.

[89] Hanford, *op. cit.*, 118; this is the period, of course, of *Of Education* and *Areopagitica*.

What does Milton answer to those who charge him with shocking impropriety? He summons his higher vision. Decorum of character, of style, decorum of genre even, are, for Milton, flexible beyond the dreams of his confuters and answerers because they are related to, take life and meaning from, a vivid concept of higher unity.

In the antiprelatical tracts, the chief image-referent was the human body. Even in description of state or church, Milton generally used the single body as metaphor. But we do have occasionally images of *bodies* as in the *Of Reformation*, where the image is of healthy and joyous physical loyalty:

Well knows every wise Nation that their Liberty consists in manly and honest labours, in sobriety and rigorous honour to the Marriage Bed, which in both Sexes should be bred up from chast hopes to loyall Enjoyments...[90]

"Rigorous honour" *and* "loyall Enjoyments" – both will remain in Milton's idea of marriage, though expanded beyond traditional interpretations. Important here is the central position of the marriage bed.

In the divorce tracts the main image is that of the man and wife in "fit conversation". The healthy, pure, free body of the antiprelatical tracts is placed in graceful conjunction with another body – another whole body, with an inside as well as an outside; the result is a new, larger, perhaps warmer harmony. The anti-image is that of the couple in loathesome conjunction, bound by custom, specious rhetoric, false decorum, canon law. This evil conjunction can be either lustful or ascetic; it is opposed to the pure and whole satisfaction of fit conversation.

Milton's scriptural authority begins in Genesis 2:18 where he finds the concept of *meet* help:

And the Lord God said, It is not good that man should be alone. I will make a helpe meet for him.

The critical term here is "helpe meet for him", and Milton glosses it at length in the *Tetrachordon*, as "effectuall conformity of disposition and affection to be heerby signify'd", as "*another self, a second self, a very self it self*".[91] The accompanying emphasis is on fit conversation with the wife, in Paraeus' words, "not as a servant, but as an undivided companion of life, that is, one who intimately lives together with him".[92] The definition of marriage is asserted again and again in these works and insists on a complicated sense of conversation, communication on many levels:

> That only then, when the minds are fitly dispos'd, and enabl'd to maintain a cherfull conversation, to the solace and love of each other, according as God intended and promis'd ... that only can be thought to be of his joyning, and not the contrary.[93]

> The full and proper and main end of mariage, is the communicating of all duties, both divine and humane, each to other, with utmost benevolence and affection.[94]

For Milton a meet help is a woman capable of rich responses to her husband, a woman capable of matchable, if not equal, mental as well as physical intercourse. The word conversation is especially apt here, as it is in Eve's speech in *Paradise Lost*, Book IV. Conversation is, according to the *NED*, "The action of consorting or having deals with others; living together; commerce, intercourse, society, intimacy". The narrower definitions given range from the purely physical to the purely mental. It is quite clear from Milton's use that for him the word has an extraordinary encompassing range. Fit conversation means the loving exchange on the appropriate levels (and assuming the inequality of the sexes)[95] of mental, physical, and spiritual comfort, solace, love.

One of the characteristics of real marriage is joy, a joy which vigorously includes the senses: "And what is life without the vigor and spiritfull exercise of life?"[96]

And Milton speaks of that "serene and blisfull condition it [marriage] was in at the beginning".[97] He vigorously defends our "need

---

[92]   Quoted in *Ibid.*, n. 40.

[93]   *Ibid.*, p. 328.

[94]   *Ibid.*, p. 465. See also pp. 608, 612. For substantiation of this definition of marriage see *De Doctrina Christiana*, Book II, chapter x. See especially pp. 121, 151, 155, 157 of volume XV of the Columbia *Milton*.

[95]   But if the woman is superior to her husband, "then a superior and more naturall law comes in, that the wiser should govern the lesse wise, whether male or female". Yale *Prose*, II, 589.

[96]   *Ibid.*, p. 274.

[97]   *Ibid.*, p. 240.

of som delightfull intermissions" and cites the allegory of the Song of Songs as singing "of a thousand raptures ... farre on the hither side of carnall enjoyment".[98] One of the climactic images of the joyous body reminds us of the earlier image of the Christian poet offering prayer:

> Every true Christian in a higher order of Priesthood is a person dedicate to joy and peace, offering himselfe a lively sacrifice of praise and thanksgiving, & there is no Christian duty that is not to be season'd and set off with cherfulnes...[99]

It is important to stress the amount of positive energy that Milton's master image here gives off, especially on a subject often cited to show what a truculent, dour, intractable man he was. Relevant to the vigor and joy of real marriage is that image, tenderly and ingenuously ambitious, of the heroic rationalist:

> I doubt not but with one gentle stroking to wipe away ten thousand teares out of the life of man. Yet thus much I shall now insist on, that what ever the institution were, it could not be so enormous, nor so rebellious against both nature and reason as to exalt it selfe above the end and person for whom it was instituted.[100]

But perhaps there is heroic mercy here, too. For although Milton is not alone in emphasizing the joyous nature of Christian marriage, he is probably the only Englishman to allow for the possible failure of marriage and to allow for divorce.

The Puritan view of marriage has been investigated by the Hallers and by Roland Mushat Frye.[101] These scholars stress the anti-ascetic attitude of the Puritans and the popularity of the subject. Frye speaks even of "the genre of Protestant marriage books".[102] Lust as a foundation for marriage was denounced, but physical love itself was celebrated as good and pure. "Love is the Marriage

---

[98] *Ibid.*, p. 597.

[99] *Ibid.*, p. 259.

[100] *Ibid.*, p. 245.

[101] William and Malleville Haller, "The Puritan Art of Love", *The Huntington Library Quarterly*, V (Jan. 1942), 235-272. William Haller, "Hail Wedded Love", *ELH*, XIII (June, 1946), 79-97. Roland Mushat Frye, "The Teachings of Classical Puritanism on Conjugal Love", *Studies in the Renaissance*, II (1955), 148-159.

[102] Frye, *op. cit.*, 149.

vertue, which singes Musicke to their whole life", Henry Smith wrote.[103] Thomas Becon's version of matrimony glows like Milton's:

One man and one woman are coupled and knit together in one fleshe and body in the feare and love of God, by the free, lovinge, harty, and good consente of them both.[104]

The Hallers suggest that it was the very magnification of the religious significance of marriage which led Puritan thought "to magnify the emotional, romantic, and idealistic aspects of the marriage relation".[105] Contemporary reactions to Milton's divorce tracts have clouded the fact that Milton starts from a conventional Puritan position:

Godliness in the heroic age of Puritanism did not necessarily spell repression and negation but quite the opposite, and, when preachers called for godliness in wives, they called women to an intensely active existence on the emotional and spiritual as well as the physical and practical level.[106]

Milton's couple in fit conversation is there physically as well as spiritually; Milton's contempt is aimed not at the body, but at the body's usurpation of a higher role than it deserves. It is the very richness of his vision which makes the argument essential.

The logical end of a high opinion of marriage, and of the emphasis on mental and spiritual fitness[107] with physical love, is that a marriage which is not "fit" should be dissolved. But only Milton did not draw back from what the Hallers call "the extreme implications"[108] of the Puritan doctrine.

If spiritual values are first in true marriage, then they should be first in the question of divorce. And if physical love is important, why condemn the unhappily married man to abstinence? The characteristic strategy of Milton's honesty is to arrange things in a hierarchy of values, and then to attend to all levels. So in the divorce tracts he insists that mental and spiritual fitness is the basis of true

---

[103] Quoted in W. and M. Haller, *op. cit.*, 258.
[104] *Ibid.*, p. 245.
[105] *Ibid.*, p. 265.
[106] *Ibid.*, p. 257.
[107] *Ibid.*, p. 258.
[108] *Ibid.*, p. 270.

marriage. Indeed the word *fitness* dominates *Tetrachordon* and always in this meaning of total compatibility with emphasis on the mental and spiritual. Without fitness the isolated fleshly act may continue,

but not holy, not pure, not beseeming the sacred bond of mariage; beeing at best but an animal excretion, but more truly wors and more ignoble then that mute kindlyness among the heards and flocks...[109]

And yet Milton's sympathy for the body is often poignant:

God loves not to plow out the heart of our endeavours with overhard and sad tasks. God delights not to make a drudge of vertue ... Forc't vertu is as a bolt overshot, it goes neither forward not backward, & does no good as it stands.[110]

Milton's attack on asceticism as a way out of the problems of marriage is more vigorous than his attack on lust:

Those commands therfore which compell us to self-cruelty above our strength, so hardly will help forward to perfection, that they hinder & set backward in all the common rudiments of Christianity...[111]

By now we arrive at a consideration of Milton's definition by opposites. With perhaps less emphasis than in the antiprelatical tracts, Milton spells out his positive vision of unity through negatives. Again we have images of excess in language and custom, illness, and imbalance in the body and in institutions. There is an extended emphasis on the disparity between inner and outer, between appearance and reality, between letter and spirit. An especial target will be over-

[109] Yale *Prose*, II, 609.
[110] *Ibid.*, p. 342.
[111] *Ibid.*, p. 331. Milton uses the tradition of Origen's self-castration with considerable effect: "And if none of these considerations with all their wait and gravity, can avail to the dispossessing him of his pretious literalism, let some one or other entreat him but to read on in the same 19. of *Math.* till he come to that place that sayes *Some make themselves Eunuchs for the kingdom of heavns sake.* And if then he please to make use of *Origens* knife, he may doe well to be his own carver" (*Ibid.*, p. 334).

See also *Colasterion*, Yale *Prose*, II, 731 : "Burdens may bee born, but still with consideration to the strength of an honest man complaining". Cf. *Tetrachordon*, Yale *Prose*, II, 689. The entire chapter x of Book II of the *De Doctrina* is of course relevant to the divorce arguments. The position is consistent with that of the tracts here under discussion, but the prose is cooler and less interesting. See Columbia *Milton* XV, 163.

literal reading of scriptural precepts that must bow to a larger law. Milton notes:

all those souls perishing by stubborn expositions of particular and inferior precepts, against the general and supreme rule of charitie.[112]

The dead letter image is used again and again: "the narrow intellectuals of quotationists and common placers",[113] "obstinate *literality*";[114] "*alphabetical* servility"[115] "the leaden daggers of your literall decrees";[116] "the gout and dropsy of a big margent, litter'd and overlaid with crude and huddl'd quotations".[117] It is a stubborn misreading of Christ which would obviate the rule of charity:

What meanes the *fanatic* boldnesse of this age that dares tutor Christ to be more strict then he thought fit?[118]

What can be more opposite and disparaging to the cov'nant of love, of freedom, & of our manhood in grace, then to bee made the yoaking pedagogue of new severities, the scribe of syllables and rigid letters, not only greevous to the best of men, but different and strange from the light of reason in them...[119]

The contempt for the "carnal textman" stays pretty constant throughout Milton's early prose. In the *Colasterion*, he ridicules his anonymous answerer:

Now hee comes to the Position, which I sett down whole; and like an able text man slits it into fowr, that hee may the better come at it with his Barbar Surgery, and his sleevs turn'd up.[120]

The dead letter is almost one with the unjust law and obsolete custom. Milton warns against "the prostrate worshippers of Custom";[121] custom, error, superstition are almost synonyms in the early prose:

---

[112]   Yale *Prose*, II, 277; see also p. 558.
[113]   *Ibid.*, p. 230.
[114]   *Ibid.*, p. 279.
[115]   *Ibid.*, p. 280.
[116]   *Ibid.*, p. 333.
[117]   *Ibid.*, p. 724.
[118]   *Ibid.*, p. 641.
[119]   *Ibid.*, p. 636.
[120]   *Ibid.*, pp. 736-737.
[121]   *Ibid.*, p. 439.

Error supports Custome, Custome count'nances Error. And these two betweene them would persecute and chase away all truth and solid wisdome out of humane life...[122]

The greatest burden in the world is superstition; not onely of Ceremonies in the Church, but of imaginary and scarcrow sins at home.[123]

As in the antiprelatical tracts one finds occasional dazzling fusions of the images of excess. At the opening of the *Doctrine and Discipline of Divorce*, Milton uses custom, illness, and false erudition:

[custom's] method is so glib and easie ... rowling up her sudden book of implicit knowledge, for him that will, to take and swallow down at pleasure; which proving but of bad nourishment in the concoction, as it was heedlesse in the devouring, puffs up unhealthily, a certaine big face of pretended learning, mistaken among credulous men, for the wholsome habit of soundnesse and good constitution.[124]

There is the accompanying assumption of the harmony of inner and outer (implicit of course in the concept of "fit conversation"). Prohibition of divorce

unties the inward knot of mariage, which is peace & love ... while it aimes to keep fast the outward formalitie...[125]

And, as always, the rigorous demand on liberty:

Just and naturall privileges man neither can rightly seek, not dare fully claime, unlesse they be ally'd to inward goodnesse...[126]

There is finally an attack on those synonyms for decorum, in their misuse; Milton speaks of "institutive decencie"[127] and "strange and lawlesse propriety".[128]

I have suggested that *Colasterion* bears the same relationship to the other divorce tracts which the *Apology* bears to the earlier antiprelatical tracts. In the last pamphlet of each series, Milton is sustaining his general polemical position but fighting in closer. He responds to the attacks on his decorum with, here, contemptuous

[122] *Ibid.*, p. 223.
[123] *Ibid.*, p. 228.
[124] *Ibid.*, pp. 222-223.
[125] *Ibid.*, p. 269.
[126] *Ibid.*, p. 587.
[127] *Ibid.*, p. 299.
[128] *Ibid.*, p. 310.

counter-attack on a narrower field. But despite the immediacy, almost intimacy, of the abuse Milton will not constrict his rhetorical terminology to the scale of his adversary. He is scornful of the servingman, for presuming beyond his station. But the freedom of his language and the virility of his own abuse, Milton defends vigorously from the example of Christ and the ethical commentators:

Hee charges mee with a *wicked gloss, and almost blasphemy,* for saying that Christ in teaching meant not always to bee tak'n word for word; but like a wise Physician administring one excess against another, to reduce us to a perfet mean. Certainly to teach thus, were no dishonest method: Christ himself hath often us'd *hyperbolies* in his teaching; and gravest Authors, both *Aristotle* in the second of his *Ethics* to *Nichomachus,* and *Seneca* in his seventh *De Beneficiis,* advise us to stretch out the line of precept oft times beyond measure...[129]

The argument about Christ's appropriateness in language is crucial, too, in the *Tetrachordon,* where Milton accuses the literal expositor of Christ's answer to the Pharisees of overturning the principles of nature, piety, and moral goodness.[130] Christ answers, Milton tells us,

in a vehement *scheme* ... And whether he suffer'd, or gave precept, being all one as was heard, it changes not the *trope* of indignation, fittest account for such askers.[131]

It is, of course, in the interest of "nature, piety, and moral goodnes"[132] that decorum of style is here invoked.

In both of these examples, and these represent the chief engagements of rhetorical decorum in the divorce tracts, Milton is arguing for a greater flexibility than his opponent can conceive of, but without moral relativism. The proper range of the arguments for truth is enormous. One is entitled to "grim laughter", the "vehement vein" if one is right, and battling wrong. One uses language appro-

---

[129] *Ibid.,* p. 745. Cf. *De Doctrina* II, x, Columbia *Milton,* XV, 159.
[130] Yale *Prose,* II, 665.
[131] *Ibid.,* p. 664.
[132] Cf. *De Doctrina,* Columbia *Milton,* XV, 159, concerning Christ's words on the hardness of their hearts: "a very appropriate answer to the Pharisees who tempted him" but not "a general explanation of the question of divorce".

priate to the subject and the occasion, but only if there is a real congruence between the language and the truth.

Proceeding on to speak of mysterious things in nature, I had occasion to fit the language therafter...[133]

But the "pork" found this "imploy'd about *a frothy, immeritous and undeserving discours*",[134] to Milton's indignation. It is the disparity between the pretence of understanding and the real understanding that Milton condemns. He moves from the style to the matter:

Such a low and home-spun expression of his Mother *English*... Nor was the stile flat and rude, and the matter grave and solid, for then ther had bin pardon, but so shallow and so unwary was that also, as gave sufficiently the character of a gross and sluggish, yet a contentious and overweening pretender.[135]

Milton's polemical guard is up here. He is more skilfully distant about his disappointment than in *An Apology*, having been able to objectify his frustration at being misunderstood in his elaborate contempt for the servingman. That same ojectivity, coolly contemptuous, is in the Sonnet "On the Detraction Which Followed Upon My Writing Certain Treatises" (Sonnet XI). But Sonnet XII is different; it expresses real disappointment and hurt in its "I did but prompt ...", in the "barbarous noise" which is structurally central, and in its admission of a miscalculation in decorum:

But this is got by casting Pearl to Hoggs.

The same sonnet, a kind of motto for the divorce tracts in its statement of the essential harmony of inner and outer asserts Christian liberty and decorum:

Licence they mean when they cry libertie;
For who loves that, must first be wise and good.[136]

The barbarous noise of those who refused to accept the dimensions

---

[133] Yale *Prose*, II, 751.
[134] *Ibid.*, p. 752.
[135] *Ibid.*, p. 725.
[136] Columbia *Milton*, I, pt. 1, 62-63.

of liberty disturbs but cannot destroy the real harmony of Milton's vision.

The attack on disharmony or spurious unity or false decorum is perhaps not so violent as the attack in the antiprelatical tracts. The same kinds of excess are attacked here as in the earlier tracts: excess in language, law or custom, erudition, ceremony. But whereas this unifying vehicle of abuse in the earliest prose was Anglican decency, in the divorce tracts it tends to be, as Kester Svendsen has pointed out, canon law.[137] And whereas the "image-referent" of the early tracts was that of the radiant singing body, here it is the rounded, spiritual and substantial couple in fit conversation. The anti-image in the earlier prose is that of the garishly dressed gabbler with a skin disease; here it is the image of "two carkasses chain'd unnaturally together; or as it may happ'n, a living soule, bound to a dead corps".[138] Nature and reason play a larger role here than in the antiprelatical tracts, but this is genuinely a question of emphasis. The basic themes are crucially related to the Christian vision of unity as the beautiful phrase "our manhood in grace" shows.

C. THE DEFENCES: THE WARFARE OF PEACE

The study of decorum in Milton's three *Defences* is met with a special set of problems. First these "pamphlets" are in Latin; a study of the Latin imagery would be presumptuous on my part. (I do not surrender a certain limited use of the imagery, or the quality of language in general, depending, I think traditionally, on the translator's mediation.) Another problem of these works, at least the *First Defence*, is the disparity between Milton's ambitious claims for the work and our feeling of disappointment at the delay, if not the squanderings, of Milton's genius. A third problem, and the most difficult perhaps, is that the comment on decorum seems less obvi-

[137]   Kester Svendsen, "Science and Structure in Milton's Doctrine of Divorce", *PMLA*, LXVII (1952), 444.
[138]   Yale *Prose*, II, 326; this is, of course, one of those times when the intense personal note makes itself felt.

ously present, at least in the form in which we encountered it in the earlier prose.

Milton has an explicit enough task: to defend a public act, the killing of a king, and later to defend the defence and the defender of the killing of a king. But as we read the pamphlets, we are shocked at Milton's political technique, and we apply our modern arsenal of logical terminology to the argument. What emerge are three gross *argumenta ad homines*. What has Salmasius' wife to do with regicide? What has Alexander More's sex life to do with the harmonious vision?

It is possible that in the very thickest parts of these problems lie some of the answers to the question: What does Milton say about decorum in these works? It is perhaps true that the answers will depend rather more on our watching the concept at work than in the earlier works. The reiterated compulsive imagery of unity and disunity in the antiprelatical and divorce tracts I see as a kind of affective statement of theme. The concept of decorum in these works is more restricted, more rigorously logical really, even when it seems most grossly illogical. Believed in, the question of a man's worthiness for his task, becomes the just center of all three works.

The question of biography is relevant here, especially in a group of works in which Milton summons his self-portrait again and again. The period after the *First Defence* was a time about which Milton wrote:

But at that time, in an especial manner, I was oppressed with concerns of a far different nature. My health was infirm, I was mourning the recent loss of two relatives, the light had now utterly vanished from my eyes. Besides, my old adversary abroad ... hovered for an attack, and now daily threatened to descend upon me with all his force.[139]

The distance between the intense suffering personal life and the public duty to which it is called is worth remembering.

The stage upon which the Defences are argued is the largest Milton ever mounted. He is defending the justice of his nation's cause, after the thrilling event of Charles' execution, against the greatest scholar in Europe and before an international audience of the

[139] *Pro Se Defensio* in Columbia *Milton*, IX, 13, 15.

learned. One can understand the grandeur of Milton's expectations. And here the Latin is appropriate; and the cadences of that Latin magnificent.

Dicam enim res neque parvas, neque vulgares; Regem potentissimum, oppressis legibus, religione afflicta, pro libidine regnantem, tandem à suo populo, qui servitutem longam servierat, bello victum...[140]

This note is struck in the second paragraph of the *Defensio Prima*; Milton in his exordium reminds his reader again and again of the mightiness of his task, "well-nigh the greatest of all subjects";[141] and he reminds us of the dangers of pride:

For what eloquence can be august and magnificent enough, what man has parts sufficient, to undertake so great a task? ... can any man have so good an opinion of himself as to think that by any style or language of his own he can compass these glorious and wonderful works – not of men, but, evidently, of almighty God?[142]

But in the first paragraph, in the first sentence, there is another note, one of contempt and personal aggrandizement. We should be prepared for the personal from the title of the work with Milton's name proudly flung. But "pride" does not really prepare a modern for the theme of scurrility, which begins immediately and is maintained pretty constantly throughout the three treatises:

If I be as copious of words and empty of matter in my Defence of the People of England as most men think Salmasius has been in his Defence of the King, I fear that I shall apparently have deserved to be called a defender at once wordy and silly.[143]

And so it starts and is continued throughout.

Milton's personal attack on Salmasius is under three headings: Salmasius is foreign and hired to do the job; Salmasius is an inadequate scholar, a garrulous rhetorician-grammarian; Salmasius is hen-pecked. Milton's national pride has been in evidence earlier, but here the term "foreigner" becomes specifically a synonym for unauthorized outsider; and combined with the fact that Salmasius

---

[140]   Columbia *Milton*, VII, 2, 4.
[141]   *Ibid.*, p. 3.
[142]   *Ibid.*, p. 7.
[143]   *Ibid.*, p. 3.

was paid to write the *Defensio Regia*, the project assumes in Milton's eyes a double moral impertinence. He accuses the "Mercenary and costly advocate"[144] of writing an exordium "most like the trumpery doleful wailings of hired mourner-women";[145] and he attacks Salmasius' "Frenchified Latin blunders".[146] Near the end of the work, Milton chastizes the English Royalists for letting "this crackbrained purse-snatcher of a Frenchman"[147] defend an English king.

Milton's attack on misused language, false rhetoric, garrulity, continues to be a major theme in the prose. In the *Defensio Prima* the attack on specious rhetoric reaches a climax. Salmasius is after all an international figure, a scholar of the first rank in reputation. But Milton tirelessly attacks the rhetorical copiousness and exaggerations of his rival. He speaks of Salmasius' "silliness and verbosity";[148] of "this outlandish rhetorician's wanton lies";[149] "this bore of a pedant, and the squallings of his professorial tongue";[150] "his counterfeit fountain of night-lucubrated tears".[151] In this work, rhetoric is used again and again pejoratively:

Mouthing your unspeakable baby-rhetoric...[152]

Ye Little Flowers of Rhetoric! (*O Flosculos!*)[153]

Your wretched bottlefuls of rhetoric-paint and fustian dye.[154]

That most egregious worn-out rhetorical cosmetic ... from the cabinets of your perfumery-shop.[155]

And Milton wants to make sure that we do not mistake garrulity for breadth:

[144]   *Ibid.*, p. 13.
[145]   *Ibid.*, p. 17.
[146]   *Ibid.*
[147]   *Ibid.*, p. 531; cf. *Defensio Secunda*, Columbia *Milton*, VIII, 139.
[148]   Columbia *Milton*, VII, 3.
[149]   *Ibid.*, p. 9.
[150]   *Ibid.*, p. 11.
[151]   *Ibid.*, p. 21.
[152]   *Ibid.*, p. 37.
[153]   *Ibid.*, pp. 40, 41.
[154]   *Ibid.*, p. 43.
[155]   *Ibid.*, p. 225. Cf. p. 343.

Nobody publishes huger dung-hills, and you deafen us all with your crowing over them...[156]

The ultimate contempt is not for the rhetorician but for the grammarian, the man concerned with the shapes of words, with words abstracted from meanings:

A learned man? – you that even unto your old age seem rather to have turned over phrase-books and lexicons and glossaries than to have perused good authors with judgment or profit; so that you prate of naught but manuscripts and various readings and dislocated passages and scribal errors... A wise man? — you that use to carry on your beggarly disputes about the meanest trifles?[157]

Whatever you touch – except when you make blunders – *is* grammar.[158]

Here, in this attack on the man with the most potent linguistic reputation in Europe, Milton presents, in action, a kind of summarizing position on language. (His treatment of Satan presents another such statement of his position.) He is not merely theoretically aware of the potential evils of language. His consistent attack on specious rhetoric, on language separated from reality of thing or feeling,[159] stretches from the *Prolusions* to the *First Defence* in a truly unbroken line. Milton was as suspicious as Plato or Aristotle of mere rhetorical efficacy. In Milton it is not the characteristic Renaissance ambiguity toward crucial terms like rhetoric, wit, decorum. Milton is more acutely aware than are his contemporaries of the possible perversions of language. I think it follows, ironically, that Milton is acutely aware of the dangers of the dissociation of sensibility.

The attack on Salmasius' relation to his wife is the most forced part of this work, though occasionally the abuse achieves some of the intended comic effect.[160] The labored puns and egregious metaphors are intended of course to demonstrate the violation of hierarchy ("decorum") in Salmasius' own home, and to extend that indecorum out to Salmasius' claim to defend the king.

[156] *Ibid.*, p. 281.
[157] *Ibid.*, p. 67.
[158] *Ibid.*, p. 69.
[159] In the *Second Defence*, Milton speaks of Salmasius as a man "absolutely without learning, if we consider things rather than words". Columbia *Milton*, VIII, 169.
[160] See for example Columbia *Milton*, VII, 349.

So this man's upside-down back-foremost mind exposes itself to either astonishment or laughter...[161]

Salmasius is a fraud, with no real inside, selling fraudulence, as in this fused image:

A landless homeless worthless straw-stuffed scarecrow-knight, selling smoke to stave off starvation in a strange land at the beck and call, and in the pay, of masters.[162]

But it is no secret that Milton called Salmasius names. The critical point is whether or not that "name-calling" had a place in this work, and for us further whether this is any kind of comment on decorum. The traditional modern attitude toward the *First Defence* is to find it "a pathetic work",[163] largely because of this scurrility. Professor Tillyard, no foe to Milton's prose, finds the *First Defence*

the longest and one of the most ephemeral of Milton's pamphlets. His furious plungings into controversy are more ridiculous than impressive. And there is an unbalanced, feverish quality in his protestations that fills the reader not with admiration but with sorrow.[164]

In this most impersonal of works, commanded by the Council of State, and in answer to a kind of abstraction of an opponent, i.e. the hired great foreign scholar, Milton rises to heights of the most personal attacks. The character of Salmasius becomes almost the chief issue. And Milton will cite his own achievement here as "the highest that I for my part have set before me in this life".[165] I cannot analyse away the disparity between Milton's attitude and my reactions. But I think that something of his attitude is explainable.

The whole idea of the worthy poet operates here. In the *First Defence*, Milton shows the impropriety, the indecorum of a foreigner, a hired man, a rhetorician, a grammarian, a sophist arguing against the English people in a matter of august dimensions. If the idea of unity and harmony between poet and poem, of congruity

---

[161]   Columbia *Milton*, VII, 211.
[162]   *Ibid.*, 33, 35.
[163]   E. M. W. Tillyard, *Milton* (London, 1951), p. 187.
[164]   *Ibid.*, p. 188. Professor Hanford concurs: "In some ways it is the least interesting and worthy of his works". Hanford, *op. cit.*, p. 141.
[165]   Columbia *Milton*, VII, 559. This passage is from the 1658 edition of the *First Defence*.

between the man praying and his prayer, between letter and spirit, inner and outer is valid, then the demand for congruity, integrity, decorum between the pleader and his cause is valid. Is this not the chief rage of the *First Defence*: that Salmasius dared to undertake the attack on the English people? And does not this rage overshadow (and it is a matter of disproportion and consequently partial failure) the legal, factual questions – though these seem to have been argued adequately enough, as contemporary opinion testifies.[166] In the face of Milton's extraordinary belief in this congruence, it is naive for us to summon terms like *argumentum ad hominem*. Milton's ideas on unity are so intense as to obviate that kind of term here.

But perhaps this matter is more clearly seen in the *Second Defence* which is in some ways, as Professor Parker says, "more a defence of Milton himself than of the English people".[167] Here along with an extraordinary attack on Alexander More we have an extraordinary defence of self, and moving addresses to Cromwell and the English people. The *Second Defence* is "successful"[168] – and partly because it gives itself more completely to the question of congruence between actor and deed. It is a study of character, praising the man who is good from within out and urging the people toward the perfection of their inner as well as outer lives. The negative corollary of course is to show that Alexander More, alleged successor to Salmasius in the controversy, is inadequate to his task of moral judgment, a contradiction to his profession. Milton is less diffuse than in the attack on Salmasius, at once more scurrilous and surer of the final use of the scurrility:

He is one "More"... A trifler, and given to women, marked also for various other offences, convicted of numerous aberrations from the orthodox faith, which he was so base as to recant on oath, and so impious as to retain...[169]

---

[166]   Hanford suggests that Milton overestimated the effects of the *First Defence* but cites many reasons for the miscalculation. *Op. cit.*, p. 14.
[167]   William Riley Parker, *Milton's Contemporary Reputation* (Columbus, 1940), p. 37.
[168]   See Tillyard, *op. cit.*, p. 194; Hanford, *op. cit.*, p. 145.
[169]   Columbia *Milton*, VIII, 31.

In an interesting echo of the doctrine of the music of the spheres Milton attacks More's use of the title *The Cry of the Royal Blood to Heaven against the English Parricides*:

Who heard this cry of the royal blood? You say that you heard it: trash! for in the first place, you are never favoured in what you hear; and the cry which ascends to heaven, if heard by any but God, is heard, as I must think, by the just and the upright alone; inasmuch as they being themselves void of offence, are authorized to denounce the wrath of God on the guilty. But to what end should you hear it? – That, lecher as you are, you might write a satire?... You have many impediments, More, you have many things ringing within and without, which will not suffer you to hear things of that nature which have reached to heaven.[170]

Is this only metaphor? Or does it represent Milton's literal views on integrity almost literally?

In contrast we have the picture of Milton, flawed by blindness now, but consistent within himself and fit for his work. In reply to the taunt about his blindness:

As for myself, I call thee, O God, to witness, the searcher of the inmost spirit, and of every thought, that I am not conscious of any offense (though, to the utmost of my power, I have often seriously examined myself on this point, though I have visited all the recesses of my heart) recently committed or long ago, the heinousness of which could have justly caused, could have called down this calamity upon me above others.[171]

This is a moving passage, one which asserts the kind of working relationship between Milton's inner and outer life. It is perhaps most touching in its demonstration that Milton expected, even from God, punishments rationally answerable to the crime.

Milton's major statement of personal integrity is the famous passage of autobiography. Just preceding the story of his life is a vivid expression of the harmony of inner and outer:

I am not such a one, who has ever disgraced fair words by foul deeds, or the language of a free man by the actions of a slave.[172]

To those whom he is defending he announces his worthiness to defend:

---

[170] *Ibid.*, pp. 45, 47.
[171] *Ibid.*, p. 67.
[172] *Ibid.*, p. 119.

That if I have ever led a life free from shame and dishonour, my defence
... can certainly never prove to them a cause of shame or disgrace. Who,
then, and whence I am I will now make known.[173]

In an era in which "images" of public figures are manipulated, indeed fabricated by barbers, tailors, speech teachers, photographers
under the direction of an image-maker hired for the purpose, the
public autobiographical statement is a joke, to be taken as seriously
as Mr. Nixon's affection for Checkers. But here Milton in a lengthy
statement soberly argues his worthiness for the task he has undertaken. It is not so surprising then to find a whole series of commentators and critics intent on smashing the Milton image, because it
claims to be not an image, but a man, not a mask, but an entity
worthy of writing great poems. It is this claim that infuriates mod-
erns, it is this claim which makes Milton so important for us.

Later, in this pamphlet, Milton praises Cromwell in the same
spirit: he argues the congruity of doer and deed, the decorum of the
whole:

[Cromwell] was a soldier, above all others the most exercised in the knowledge of himself; he had either destroyed, or reduced to his own control,
all enemies within his breast – vain hopes, fears, desires. A commander
first over himself, the conqueror of himself, it was over himself he had
learnt most to triumph.[174]

To Fairfax, Milton repeats some of the same praise, the conquest
of the inner as well as the outer:

It is not the enemy alone, you have conquered; you have conquered ambition, and what itself conquers the most excellent of mortals, you have
conquered glory.[175]

And finally, and most amazingly in its candor and vision, the address to the English people asks for consistency of inner and outer:

Unless your liberty be of that kind, which can neither be gotten, nor taken
away by arms; and that alone is such, which, springing from piety, justice,
temperance, in fine, from real virtue, shall take deep and intimate root in
your minds; you may be assured, there will not be wanting one, who,
even without arms, will speedliy deprive you of what it is your boast to

---

[173]   *Ibid.*
[174]   *Ibid.*, p. 215.
[175]   *Ibid.*, pp. 217, 219.

have gained by force of arms... Unless by real and sincere devotion to God and man, not an idle and wordy, but an efficacious, an operative devotion, you drive from your minds superstition, which originates in an ignorance of true and substantial religion, you will not want those who will sit upon your backs... Unless you banish avarice, ambition, luxury from your thoughts, and all excess even from your families, the tyrant, whom you imagined was to be sought abroad, and in the field, you will find at home, you will find within, and that a more inexorable one; yea, tyrants without number will be daily engendered in your own breasts, that are not to be borne. Conquer these first; this is the warfare of peace...[176]

This splendid admonition to know thyself animates the whole of the *Second Defence* and less purely but nevertheless vehemently the *First Defence* and the *Author's Defence of Himself*. And whereas, for us, "Know Thyself" means "Learn to Put Up With Yourself", to Milton it meant "Make Thyself Whole".

The discussion of character wholeness dominates this tract. The questions of state fact are absorbed in the discussion of integrity, largely argued on personal grounds. But it is not, finally, personalities in which Milton is indulging. It is the idea of wholeness, of Decorum, using personal examples. And is this not a characteristic of the prose? Milton will argue vehemently over large ideas. He will use "personal" examples, not precise logical terms but images of similar nature and images of opposing natures. But these groups of loosely-connected images make consistent sense only if they are seen to explicate the one master idea. A further complication is that the master idea receives its fullest statement *as* image; this master image-idea is sometimes explicit only in its parts. To visualize it is impossible; to pursue it as an *idea* in the modern sense in logical development is impossible. Somewhere between and above the realm of image and idea, perhaps in a fusion of the two, hovers the Miltonic unity, the concept of decorum. It is only in this way that we can account for the emblematic dominance of Milton's vision of himself:

I shall surpass no less the orators of all ages in the nobleness and in the instructiveness of my subject. This it is, which has imparted such expectation, such celebrity to this theme, that I now feel myself not in the forum

[176]   *Ibid.*, pp. 239, 241.

or on the rostrum, surrounded by a single people only, whether Roman or Athenian, but, as it were, by listening Europe, attending, and passing judgment... I imagine myself to have set out upon my travels, and that I behold from on high, tracts beyond the seas, and wide-extended regions; that I behold countenances strange and numberless, and all, in feelings of mind, my closest friends and neighbours.[177]

"Feelings of mind" (*animi sensus*); Milton would have provided Mr. Eliot with the phrase, had the latter looked sympathetically. And somewhere in this area between image and idea lie the areas of investigation most likely to show how Milton's decorum works. It is this area between image and idea that has yielded so much to A. E. Barker and Kester Svendsen in their studies of the prose and to D. C. Allen and Arnold Stein in their studies of the poetry. These men have not only identified major ideas in Milton but taken them seriously enough to perceive how subtly and variously the ideas work in images. If one sacrifices certain "modern" questions on anachronism while watching that unity work, it is only in the interests of allowing the works their full statement for the present. If we suspend our commitments to the necessity for modern logical and psychological dissection and comment would we see as the most significant factor in the Defences Milton's egregious egoism and bad manners? Or would we see Milton's insistence on an ultimate *decorum personae*: a man must be worthy of his life, of the tasks he undertakes, of the words he uses.

In the *Pro Se Defensio* we are given again and again the idea of worthiness in pure form:

It is not the tongue, it is not the voice only of a man which speaks; his life, his manners, his actions, more frequently when the tongue is silent, cry aloud and testify all that any one could desire.[178]

Following this statement of principle, Milton launches into a defence of his language, his digressions and other procedure in the *Second Defence*.[179] As part of the argument for a larger decorum he will use the smaller decorum cuttingly in his defence of himself.

---

[177] *Ibid.*, p. 13.
[178] Columbia *Milton*, IX, 81.
[179] *Ibid.*, p. 85.

I was not so ignorant of decorum [*decori nescius*], as to place, in a history of you, any thing either sublime or tragic.[180]

You say I promised the ambassador, "that nothing indecorous [*indecens*] should fall from my pen"; – And I have not deceived him; or, if I have at all offended in this respect, I have offended against myself only, while employed in shaking off those loathsome odours of yours, and in handling your pollutions: and, as I said before in my preface, I considered less what might most become me, than what was best suited to you [*non tam quid me magis decuisset, quam quid te dignum esset spectabam*].[181]

Then he defends himself on the authority of "those grave orators of old". Following the pattern set in the other two groups of tracts, there is, in the last of the series, more attention paid to rhetorical matters and along traditional lines. In the *Pro Se*, Milton cites Piso, Sallust, Herodotus, Suetonius, Plutarch, Erasmus, Sir Thomas More, Clemens Alexandrinus, Arnobius, Lactantius, Eusebius, Moses, Solomon, Cicero, Plautus and "the Socratic philosophers". Milton is obviously serious about his authorities; but at the end he returns to his main theme:

Let us hear no more then, most polluted man, of your trifling about the honorable and the becoming [*de honesto & decoro*]; believe me, this becomes not you; nay, be assured, there is nothing less becoming, nothing more foreign to the very nature of decorum, than for such a one as you to usurp the language of purity, or to censure that which is foul.[182]

Later, Milton writes:

You honour [Calvin] as a prophet by erecting a monument [an oration] to him, while you stab him with your life and manners...[183]

It is consistent for Milton to present here the harmonious relation of doer and deed as essential, as he presented the relation of poet and poem in his early work. And consistent too is the reiteration, on the highest classical authority, of the propriety of "vehement expressions", "grim laughter". Here Milton cites Plato and the Socratic Philosophers "that there was nothing more appropriate, more suitable to decorum, than the intermixture – the sprinklings of wit on the gravest subjects".[184]

[180]   *Ibid.*, p. 97.
[181]   *Ibid.*, p. 107.
[182]   *Ibid.*, p. 113.
[183]   *Ibid.*, p. 127.
[184]   *Ibid.*, p. 177.

I have not here undertaken a rhetorical analysis of the *Defences*, though such an analysis would demonstrate Milton's command and exercise of classical principles. Milton himself speaks of these principles many times, defending his exordium, his digressions, his style. I have chosen to emphasize what I think more important as a governing principle in the work, the concept of *decorum personae* in its widest sense. In the *Defences*, we have Milton vigorously exploiting the range of rhetoric, most notably the outer reaches of scurrility. At the same time he asserts again and again that word and thing must be related, that the orator must be worthy of his oration,[185] that there must be a correspondence and harmony in the rhetorical performance, of speaker, subject, word. The vituperation is against the fact of the fragmented or hypocritical self.

But alas! wretch that you are! you have long been at dreadful variance with yourself! To you, nothing is more intolerable than to be, to dwell with yourself…[186]

The emblem of the pretentious and divided self, of More, half-lecher, half-spiritual minister (in the *First Defence*, of Salmasius, half "authority", half timid bore) dominates the Defences. And the opposite emblem is the one of Milton, Cromwell, the English people, in ascending tones of exultation, acting as the teachers to the world, whole radiant figures representing the nation under God, virtuous in the classical sense:

Indeed, as the reproof of the bad is meant as a most serious punishment, so is the commendation of the good intended as the noblest reward; it is not merely just – it goes near to the perfection of justice: we may add, that, in the just regulation of life, we see they are both almost of equal efficacy. In effect, these two things are so closely allied, that they are accomplished by one and the same act: for when we blame the bad, we may be considered, in some sort, as praising the good.[187]

[185]   The classical sources of this are explored in Irene Samuel, *Plato and Milton* (Ithaca, 1947), pp. 45-67. Milton has of course made his major statement of the poet as "himself … a true Poem" in *An Apology*, Yale *Prose*, I, 890. (See note 121, which refers to a related passage in *Prolusion* VI, Yale *Prose*, I, 266, and a similar statement in "Familiar Letter No. 23" to Henry De Brass; Columbia *Milton*, XII, 93.) For Cicero's cited concurrence see *Prolusion* VII, Yale *Prose*, I, 288.
[186]   Columbia *Milton*, IX, 189.
[187]   *Ibid.*, p. 223.

We know good through knowing evil. We know wholeness by knowing fragmentation. We must assume that these massive reiterations are really what Milton means rather than mere politically adept statements. Within the province of those two statements, Milton's range is fantastic – various, violent, and subtle. The basic principle of the prose we have examined is beautiful unity – decorum, with Milton insistent that the principle is both universal and private; indeed personal decorum, variety with wholeness, freedom with responsibility, is the beginning and end of society. Our emblem moved from the poet, to the couple, to the prophet, not to the elaborate social structure. This is in itself consistent with the movement of Milton's thought through to the last poems; the enthusiasm for social organization and for exterior form is always conjoined with scrupulous demands upon the individual self.

D.   THAT SUBLIME ART

It is quite possible to accept this view of Milton's intense ardor toward unity and yet deny that this is decorum. Milton has used the term with considerable circumscription in parts of the prose, and I think it essential for me to make connections between these limited uses of the word and the large implications of the word for which I argue above.

Milton's most intriguing statement on decorum, and the one on which critics have seized for the widest implications is the statement in *Of Education*. In the description of that awesome curriculum, ✓ Milton finally arives at

that sublime art which in *Aristotles poetics*, in *Horace*, and the *Italian* commentaries of *Castelvetro, Tasso, Mazzoni*, and others, teaches what the laws are of a true *Epic* poem, what of a *Dramatic*, what of a *Lyric*, what decorum is, which is the grand master peece to observe. This would make them soon perceive what despicable creatures our common rimers and play-writes be, and shew them, what Religious, what glorious and magnificent use might be made of Poetry both in divine and humane things. From hence and not till now will be the right season of forming them to be able writers and composers in every excellent matter, when they shall be thus fraught with an universall insight into things.[188]

Modern critics have made this passage do considerable duty. They have especially used the phrase "grand master peece to observe" to indicate Milton's commitment to a rhetorical tradition capable of broad applications.[189] But the word *master peece* itself is pejorative in other uses in Milton and in contemporary usage among the Puritans; it may perhaps be closer to the meaning of the modern word *gimmick* than to guiding principle.[190] And this strikes me as rather more consistent with the practical rushed tone of the ambitiousness in *Of Education*. In any case, I think it not valid to set up the phrase "decorum, the grand master peece", as some final proof of the scope of the term in Milton. This decision leaves me with no use of the term *decorum* in the large sense which I have described.

In most uses of the word in English, Milton means by decorum, *decorum personae*; he means consistency of speech and action to the character. Ida Langdon, the first person to localize the problem in any way, agrees that it was "in the sense of typical fitness ... that Milton ordinarily interpreted 'decorum' and placed it among the 'masterpieces' – matters of high importance to be observed in studying or writing poetry".[191] This typical fitness, Miss Langdon traces back through Minturno, not to Aristotle's general term but to "the four Aristotelian requirements for tragic character...".[192]

Of the passages in which Milton discusses *decorum personae*, I have not much more to say than Miss Langdon or Professor Svendsen in his article on the subject.[193] I have pointed out the passage in *An Apology* and shown that, in contrast with Milton's argument for

---

[188] Yale *Prose*, II, 404-406. This is one of the most documented passages in Milton's prose (see e.g. the notes in the edition cited), but there are still questions in my mind, even of simple pronoun reference.

[189] See for example Merritt Hughes in his edition of Milton's *Prose Selections* (New York, 1947), p. 45; Kester Svendsen, "Epic Address and Reference and the Principle of Decorum in *Paradise Lost*", *Philological Quarterly*, XXVIII (1949), 186.

[190] For documentation see my "Milton's 'grand master peece'", *American Notes & Queries*, II (1963), 54-55.

[191] Ida Langdon, *op cit.*, p. 112.

[192] *Ibid.*

[193] Svendsen, "Epic Address".

broad freedom of language this passage assails his opponent with the charge of miscalling the Parliament a Convocation. In *Eikonoklastes*, Milton in speaking of the piety of Charles says:

The Poets also, and som English, have bin in this point so mindfull of *Decorum*, as to put never more pious words in the mouth of any person, then of a Tyrant.[194]

Milton then cites the piety which Shakespeare puts in the mouth of Richard III, and commends him for observance of decorum.

One of the most telling technical points against Salmasius and the most extended of Milton's comments on *decorum personae* is the passage in Chapter V of the *First Defence*. Salmasius had cited Aeschylus in *The Suppliants* as calling the king of the Argives "a ruler not subject to judgment". Efficiently and completely, but without use of the term itself, Milton shows that the words are spoken by the fifty daughters of Danaus and hence are the words of both strangers and suppliants and not to be taken for the words of the playwright. Milton accuses Salmasius of being "recklessly uncritical" and proceeds to state the principle of *decorum personae*:

Know then ... that we must not regard the poet's words as his own, but consider who it is that speaks in the play, and what that person says; for different persons are introduced, sometimes good, sometimes bad, sometimes wise men, sometimes fools, and they speak not always the poet's own opinion, but what is most fitting to each character.[195]

In the *Second Defence* there is some slight expansion of the term. Milton sets up an interesting parody of Salmasius, More, and Vlaccus in terms of a trumpery tragedy, then proceeds to defend his style in the *First Defence*:

If any one should think our refutation deficient in gravity, he should consider that we have not to do with a grave adversary, but with a herd of players; to which, while it was necessary to accommodate the nature of the refutation, we thought it proper to have in view not always what would be most suitable to decorum, but what would most suit them.[196]

194   Columbia *Milton*, V, 84. The passage, once thought to be an attack on Shakespeare, has been shown to be otherwise. See Langdon, *op. cit.*, p. 114.
195   Columbia *Milton*, VII, 307. Compare 327 of the same volume: "poets generally put something like their own opinions into the mouths of their best characters".
196   Columbia *Milton*, VIII, 45.

Here decorum means fitness of style to author, and is opposed to fitness of style to character speaking. But there is the added metaphorical perspective of the "play" which may have some influence here. Two pages later, Milton is back to the strict sense, accusing Salmasius of being

> so ignorant of every thing that is called decorum... as to suffer opinions, which he thought becoming [*decere*] in an honest and prudent person, to be put into the mouth of a man who is an arrant scoundrel.[197]

And somewhat between the two positions is the third mention in this work:

> The poet [who praised Salmasius] too must have been a sorry poet, and unobservant of decorum [*indecorus*] who could dignify with such immoderate eulogiums a grammarian, – a description of person, who has ever been a menial – merely subservient to poets.[198]

These speeches are all but one consistent with *decorum personae*. In the *History of Britain*, the single mention of decorum is less easily categorized. In retelling the story of Boadicea, Milton condemns those historians who melodramatized her in battle, to the shame of the British:

> I affect not set speeches in a Historie, unless known for certain to have bin so spok'n in effect as they are writ'n, nor then, unless worth rehearsal; and to invent such, though eloquently ... is an abuse of posteritie ... Much less therefore do I purpose heer or elsewhere to Copie out tedious Orations without decorum, though in thir Authors compos'd ready to my hand.[199]

Here we assume that, in history, decorum is the relevant and actual words of a character; a dramatically consistent but unfactual speech is "without decorum".

There is one quite simple reference to decorum in the *Christian Doctrine*; here the term has the restrictiveness of our modern usage of it. In speaking of modesty, Milton writes:

[197]   *Ibid.*, pp. 49, 51. A further problem is translation. I have been following the listing in the Columbia *Index* on these pages. But the editors are inconsistent, citing some but not all of the occurrences of the term. The noun appears several times in Latin, but not cited in the *Index*.
[198]   Columbia *Milton*, VIII, 81.
[199]   Columbia *Milton*, X, 68.

MODESTY consists in refraining from all obscenity of language or action, in short, from whatever is inconsistent with the strictest decency of behaviour in reference to sex or person... The same ideas of womanly decorum existed even among the Gentiles.[200]

This could be taken from Dr. Johnson or Jane Austen. It is interesting that it should be couched in negatives.

One of the few times when Milton uses *decency* with the full force of a synonym for decorum is in that passage of intensive reflection on genre and style in *The Reason for Church-government*. Milton attacks

libidinous and ignorant Poetasters, who having scars ever heard of that which is the main consistence of a true poem, the choys of such persons as they ought to introduce, and what is morall and decent to each one, doe for the most part lap up vitious principles in sweet pils to be swallow'd down...[201]

This is, very clearly, *decorum personae*.

The uses of decorum in the *Pro Se Defensio* I have examined just above.[202] Here is a vigorous defence of personal style having to do largely with propriety of style to subject (i.e. "base" in this instance) and the propriety of mixing wit with serious matters. This latter leads us to a consideration of Milton's oft-cited strictness in decorum and the relation of the two decorums. Indeed, this position on wit which has been cited again and again in this study, serves as the bridge between the two decorums.

Milton is very much aware of rhetorical precepts on decorum; he is aware of *decorum personae*; of the three styles, lofty, mean, and low; of the traditional demands of genre, the "kinds". Each of these aspects of decorum is obviously worthy of a full study; each of these Milton has commented on; and each of these, especially the last, is important in viewing the poetry. I am conscious of having skirted the generic questions Milton raises in *The Reason of*

---

[200] Columbia *Milton*, XVII, 221. See also p. 223 for comments on decorum in dress. Decency consists in "refraining from indecorum or lasciviousness in dress or personal appearance".

[201] Yale *Prose*, I, 818.

[202] I have not noted all the uses, but those remaining instances on 103 and 113 of Columbia *Milton*, IX, are consistent with usages described above.

Church-government and *Of Education.* I am aware of possibly important answers to these questions. But I have been governed in my
study of this prose by the conviction that the "decorums" imply a
Decorum; and Milton himself in his insistence on the theme of language has created my conviction.

Milton attacks over-elaborate, pretentious language steadily,
from the time of the Prolusions through to *Samson Agonistes.* In
this attack, Milton insists that exterior propriety is not enough. It
must be allied in a proper way to inner purity. Therefore, when he
attacks his opponents on the grounds of *decorum personae*, I see
this attack as subsumed under a larger concept, even when the two
concepts would seem, temporarily, to clash. I cannot conceive how
Milton could use the term decorum in a limited sense without being
conscious of its subservience to a higher use. When in *Eikonoklastes*, for example, Milton speaks of the decorum of the pious words
of Shakespeare's Richard III, it is immediately after an attack on the
private Psalter of Charles I:

Which they who so much admire, either for the matter or the manner, may
as well admire the Arch-Bishops late Breviary, and many other as good
Manuals, and *Handmaids of Devotion*, the lip-work of every Prelatical
Liturgist, clapt together, and quilted out of Scripture phrase, with as
much ease, and as little need of Christian diligence, or judgement, as be-
longs to the compiling of any ord'nary and salable peece of English
Divinity, that the Shops value. But he who from such a kind of Psalmist-
ry, or any other verbal Devotion, without the pledge and earnest of suta-
ble deeds, can be perswaded of a zeale, and true righteousness in the person, hath much yet to learn.[203]

In this instance, decorum becomes a technical term for praising
Shakespeare's insight in presenting a common fraud. My point is
that of the two discussions of language, the one just quoted seems
to me the more important, the one dominating the ensuing statement on Shakespeare's observance of decorum. So it is throughout
the pamphlets; the attacks on the modest confuter's use of *convocation*,[204] on Hall's misuse of *satire*,[205] on Salmasius' misuse of
Aeschylus is always imbedded in a general attack on misuse (shall

---

[203]   Columbia *Milton*, V, 83-84.
[204]   See above, p. 66.
[205]   *Ibid.*

I say insincerity?) of language – the disharmony of word and spirit, of inner and outer.

Milton's larger idea of order and consistency dominates his views on rhetorical decorum to the extent that his own times thought him improper and our time thought him dissociated. Steadily throughout the controversial pamphlets answering him runs the accusation of indecorum, of excess in language. Are the accusers simply repeating Milton's argument? No, because they lack the comprehensiveness, the radiance and breadth of Milton's master concept-image. In general, Milton is accused of being improper, while Milton accuses his enemies of being *wrong*. To ignore this distinction, or to try to attribute Milton's judgment to peevishness, intolerance, or personal inadequacy is to ignore the whole vast complexity of his language itself.

We have already seen what Thomas Fuller thought of Milton's attack on the bishops.[206] The modest confuter speaks of Milton's "lewd profanations, scurrilous jests, slanderous and reproachfull calumnies".[207] The servingman against divorce advised Milton:

Is this the fine language that your Book is commended for: Good your worship look a little upon your Rhetorick.... What a Boarish Adjective you joyne with a Polititian.[208]

The writer of the *Censure of the Rota* speaks of the *First Defence* as "that admired piece, which you writ to confute his Wife and his Maid".[209] Shortly before, an anonymous pamphlet had attacked Milton as:

[The] Goos-quill Champion, who had need of *a Help meet* to establish any thing ... he is so much an enemy to usual practices, that I believe when he is condemned to travel to *Tyburn* in a Cart, he will petition for the favour to be the first man that ever was driven thither in a *Wheel-bar-row*...[210]

[206]   See above, p. 64.
[207]   *A Modest Confutation of a Slanderous and Scurrilous Libell entituled Animad-versions etc.* (London, 1642), p. 1, printed in Parker, *op. cit.*
[208]   *An Answer to a Book, Intituled The Doctrine and Discipline of Divorce etc.* (London, 1644), p. 17, printed in Parker, *op. cit.*
[209]   *The Censure of the Rota Upon Mr. Miltons Book Entituled The Ready and Easy Way To Establish A Free Common-wealth* (London, 1660), p. 4; in Parker, *op. cit.*
[210]   Quoted in Parker, *op. cit.*, p. 99.

These are strange comments on a man "with strict views of decorum in speech and composition",[211] a man conscious of decorum, "no man more so". Either Milton was unsuccessful in observing decorum or he observed a decorum larger than or different from many of his contemporaries.

It is through his defences of the violent style, in *Of Reformation*, *Animadversions*, *An Apology*, *Colasterion*, the *Second Defence*, the *Defence of Himself* that Milton seeks to link the two decorums. Milton insists on *decorum personae* in the moral sense. If a man is bad and claims to be worthy of moral statement, he may be impugned in any terms. If a man, on the other hand, is good and arguing for the good, he is free of the necessity of ordinary niceness. The decorous Christian is the one who has great flexibility of expression but no moral relativism. (And even this needs a footnote: I have demonstrated Milton's measured tolerance of the weaknesses of flesh as flesh.)

Milton's images of unity dominate and *direct* the prose. It is the fact that they function as directors that allow me to call this vision of unity decorum. It is not only that Milton is "unusually, even heretically explicit in his denial of dualism",[212] and assertion of the unity of the human:

Man is a living being, intrinsically and properly one and individual, not compound or separable, not, according to the common opinion, made up and framed of two distinct and different natures, as of soul and body, but ... the whole man is soul, and the soul man, that is to say, a body, or substance individual, animated, sensitive, and rational.[213]

This is an image; the dynamic application of the image is decorum, as in the opening of *The Tenure of Kings and Magistrates*:

If men within themselves would be govern'd by reason, and not generally give up thir understanding to a double tyrannie, of Custom from without and blind affections within, they would discerne better, what it is to favour and uphold the Tyrant of a Nation. But being slaves within doors, no wonder that they strive so much to have the public State conformably

[211]   *Ibid.*, p. 269.
[212]   Isabel Gamble MacCaffrey, *Paradise Lost as 'Myth'* (Cambridge, 1959), p. 66.
[213]   Columbia *Milton*, XV, 41.

govern'd to the inward vitious rule, by which they govern themselves.[214]

Or consider the dynamism and the power of rhetorical direction of these image-concepts in *Areopagitica*:

It was from out the rinde of one apple tasted, that the knowledge of good and evill as two twins cleaving together leapt forth into the World. And perhaps this is that doom which *Adam* fell into of knowing good and evill, that is to say of knowing good by evill.[215]

And at the end of the lovely allegory of Truth, we have an application of the allegory, both emblem and operation:

To be still searching what we know not, by what we know, still closing up truth to truth as we find it (for all her body is *homogeneal*, and proportionall) this is the golden rule in *Theology* as well as in *Arithmetick*, and makes up the best harmony in a Church; not the forc't and outward union of cold, and neutrall, and inwardly divided minds.[216]

This is my apology for finding Decorum not in the indexed places, but in the master-images and themes of the prose. If I find Milton using the term in its restrictive sense, I can only say that it is almost always imbedded in a context which asserts the larger concept. In this analysis I am of course conscious of overemphases: I do not claim a perfect Milton. The *First Defence* strikes me as unsuccessful in many ways. But the idea of viewing it as a discussion of character and its worthiness to action does I think help to see the work more completely and it is consistent with ideas developed throughout the prose. The same I find is true of the other prose works, including the *Areopagitica*. The decorum I argue for invests Milton's prose; it does not render that prose perfect.

The concept of decorum operates like those other master concepts in Milton, Christian liberty and temperance. In a sense, all three concepts are ways of looking at a central truth, "homogeneal and proportionall". All three function as a kind of end as well as a means. All three govern minor versions of themselves. All three contain the fierce equation of the living and the received in a tension which gives luminousness to the harmonious vision. The best

---

[214] Columbia *Milton*, V, 1.
[215] Yale *Prose*, II, 514.
[216] *Ibid.*, 551.

scholarship and criticism of our day has recognized the dynamism of Milton's visions of unity. Some of these recognitions I will discuss in the chapters to follow.

I now read with sympathy and a remarkable degree of concurrence Milton's claims in the *Second Defence*:

Reflecting, therefore, that there are in all three species of liberty, without which it is scarcely possible to pass any life with comfort, namely, ecclesiastical, domestic or private, and civil; that I had already written on the first species, and saw the magistrate diligently employed about the third, I undertook the domestic, which was the one that remained.[217]

Milton changed his mind about Presbyterians, Mary Powell, and Parliament, but the basic integrity of his statement stands. Milton's prose is not monolithic, nor are his attitudes to the problems of his world unchanging. But consistent and vibrant throughout the prose we have examined is his vision of unity; consistent too is a method of operation which attempts always to close up truth to truth to recreate the vision in reality.

In a very profound sense, Milton spoke truth about himself.

My definition of Milton's concept of decorum, arrived at after reading the prose, is this: Decorum is a concept of harmonious, resonant, joyous unity, with consistency of inner and outer and enormous variety and range extending from a base of certainty about the ends of discourse and indeed of all human "conversation". Decorum is an idea of unity which inspires and governs the operations of life and writing. Decorum includes other "decorums", the "rules", of genre, style, and characterization, but it is characterized by a flexibility without relativism, by intricate and dynamic relationships between parts, indeed opposites, the very tensions of which give luminosity.

This is the definition I find implicit in the prose I have examined. The complexity need not disturb the unity any more than the amazing images of excess in the antiprelatical tracts were the less cohesive for being elaborate fusions of kinds of excesses. This is the concept which I believe I have shown derives from the prose. It is possible, I think, to show that the concept operates in the verse also.

[217]   Columbia *Milton*, VIII, 131.

III. DECORUM IN THE VERSE

A. DECORUM IN MILTON'S VERSE

If Milton's vision of radiant unity is not only an end, in psychological and religious terms, but a means toward that end, a method of closing up truth to truth, it should be an illuminating factor in reading the poems. If my claims for Milton's decorum are just, that decorum should be applicable to the verse without distortion of the latter; and where the verse contains "problems", i.e. loci of alleged thinness, excess, or inconsistency, Milton's decorum may help illuminate the problem. I do not intend to use decorum as a pair of rose-colored glasses, and I am aware of the possibility of question-begging. But surely sensitivity to Milton's ideal of wholeness and to his motion toward that wholeness ought to make us sensitive to both large structural patterns and details of texture.

Perhaps I am trying here to displace one decorum with another, the modern with the Miltonic. For surely there is a modern decorum in Milton criticism and surely that is what is being summoned by Mr. John Peter when he asks somewhat querulously:

Why in view of his utter disregard for Sin (790-809), should Death pay any attention to her admonition to restrain his fury (734-5)? Does he foolishly expect her to keep the gates locked, despite her obvious and avowed intention (856-63) of disobeying him? Or is he less fool than knave, an intriguer waiting to trap Satan — and perhaps Man too – after they have been opened? ... as well as praising him for giving her life (864-5) would Sin not feel resentful towards Satan for giving her such a Son?

Why should he [God] find it necessary to hoodwink his own angels?[1]

[1]   John Peter, *A Critique of Paradise Lost* (New York, 1960), p. 48.

It is not only the tone of surface and induced indignation which is objectionable here. It is the setting up of a decorum of "psychological" backing up and filling in which is a cliché of sophomore creative writing nurtured on the fiction of the nineteenth and early twentieth century. It is a criticism as hidebound in its insistence on modern motivation as seventeenth century critics (say Thomas Rymer) were in their insistence on *decorum personae*.

The source of much of this, indignation and cliché, is A. J. A. Waldock's often cited *Paradise Lost and Its Critics*.[2] In this hostile book, Professor Waldock has ignored Milton's vision of unity, the ideal of the rounded and religious man, for *his* ideal, the "natural" man. Our active and imaginative acceptance of the idea of wholeness gives way to concern for the fuzzy and sentimental area of fallen man's existence. It is this stubbornly maintained rule of the "natural" man by which we are to measure each speech in *Paradise Lost*. Professor Waldock is insistent on decorum, his decorum of the natural man. "Naturally", Professor Waldock keeps saying – but that nature which he assumes in his reader is too limited for Milton. Quite clearly Milton's idea of wholeness absorbs Waldock's naturalness; and quite clearly that Miltonic decorum is more natural in the human sense than Mr. Waldock's or Mr. Peter's nuggets of motivation.

We can see the problems created when the decorum of naturalistic fiction is applied to *Paradise Lost*, when Waldock writes that in Book IX, lines 1182 ff. Milton is "himself more thoroughly *with* Adam" than anywhere else in the poem, "he is bitterly, weepingly with him".[3] This is a strong statement and it is nonsense. I do not find this intense identification in the verse, though I am sure it could be imported from the Milton reputation. Nor do I find the climax of the poem, in Waldock's sense, when Adam decides to fall with Eve. That great and moving scene can work on us but need not finally win us. The emphasis is Mr. Waldock's, not Milton's, consciously or unconsciously, and Mr. Waldock is emphasizing in

[2] A. J. A. Waldock, *Paradise Lost and Its Critics* (Cambridge, 1959). See especially "The Fall (II)", pp. 42-64, where "natural", "naturally", and "Everybody admits it" justify the critical judgments.
[3] *Ibid.*, p. 34.

the name of a natural reader whom I find unnatural and limited.
Fifteen years ago, Professor Woodhouse wrote on nature and grace.
His comments are still relevant:

[Amoret's] education has failed to unite the human virtue of chastity to
the natural principle of generation because it has failed to recognize that
on the human level the virtue is as natural as the principle...[4]

Professor Waldock argues as though virtue were not natural for the
human being. He substitutes for love under God the primacy of
domestic relations, and domestic relations in no pure sense (surely
not in the magnificent sense of Book IV). He operates in the thinner
area of human relations. What he gives up "naturally" I am not
willing to lose: our manhood in grace, the splendor of wedded love
under God; and he gives up, with Mr. Peter, the great poem in
exchange for the crucially flawed poem, the great children's
poem. I prefer Milton's version of what is natural to the human,
and I think it more accurate than Professor Waldock's. And I prefer Milton's *Paradise Lost*.

B. THE ECCENTRICAL EQUATION

The place in which to view, in a kind of final emblematic way, the
harmonious vision, the rich visualization of unity, is in Heaven.
But Satan is not alone in sneering at the order in heaven. Professor
Rajan writes:

That voice which in 'Of Reformation' was preparing to celebrate God's
mercies can sing only in bleak and barren measures against the tepid
hymns and hallelujahs of the saints.[5]

---

[4]   A. S. P. Woodhouse, "Nature and Grace in *The Faerie Queene*", *ELH*, XVI
(1949), 217. The comment by Roland M. Frye is also relevant: "Satan's appeal
to Eve is not that she should be natural, but rather that she should be supernatural, and her fall comes in attempting to ascend". *God, Man, and Satan*
(Princeton, 1960), p. 54.
[5]   B. Rajan, *Paradise Lost and the Seventeenth Century Reader* (New York,
1948), p. 129. But compare Professor Rajan's sympathetic and I think relevant
comment on the dance as a form of world order: "You need the dance to suggest
the union of ecstasy with control, the underlying discipline which animates the
universe". *Ibid.*, p. 53.

Milton, characteristically, provides us with critical terms in Satan's sardonic words to Abdiel before the first day's battle in Heaven:

> At first I thought that Libertie and Heav'n
> To heav'nly Soules had bin all one; but now
> I see that most through sloth had rather serve,
> Ministring Spirits, traind up in Feast and Song;
> Such hast thou arm'd, the Ministrelsie of Heav'n,
> Servilitie with freedom to contend,
> As both thir deeds compar'd this day shall prove.
>
> (*PL* VI, 164-170)[6]

Satan is no fool here; he demands our attention and not only toward himself. We are called upon to weigh the charge of "Ministrelsie". We are called on to evaluate the "song and dance" of Heaven. Abdiel's answer is a shrewd one, interestingly noting Satan's self-love, but behind the good angel's argument lies the earlier vision of the angels in heaven; that image must be strong enough to support Abdiel's argument here and to disprove Satan's or the scene is dramatically inept, a manipulated failure. If Satan is successful in challenging the order of heaven, this passage is indecorous: it violates the higher unity of the poem for a momentary effect.

The order of Heaven has been earlier established and not as a rigid and dry, a servile and joyless, order. I do not deny the absoluteness of obedience, but the vision itself is of a dynamic, moving unity, not of a flat geometric order. In Book III, after Christ's momentous acceptance of the Incarnation, God bids the angels "Adore the Son, and honour him as mee". The angels oblige:

> No sooner had th'Almighty ceas't, but all
> The multitude of Angels with a shout
> Loud as from numbers without number, sweet
> As from blest voices, uttering joy, Heav'n rung
> With Jubilee, and loud Hosanna's filld
> Th' eternal Regions: lowly reverent
> Towards either Throne they bow, and to the ground
> With solemn adoration down they cast
> Thir Crowns inwove with Amarant and Gold,
> Immortal Amarant, a Flour which once
> In Paradise, fast by the Tree of Life
> Began to bloom, but soon for mans offence

[6]   The question has been raised earlier of course in Book II, 239-249.

To Heav'n remov'd where first it grew, there grows,
And flours aloft shading the Fount of Life,
And where the river of Bliss through midst of Heavn
Rowls o're *Elisian* Flours her Amber stream;
With these that never fade the Spirits elect
Bind thir resplendent locks inwreath'd with beams,
Now in loose Garlands thick thrown off, the bright
Pavement that like a Sea of Jasper shon
Impurpl'd with Celestial Roses smil'd.
Then Crown'd again thir gold'n Harps they took,
Harps ever tun'd, that glittering by thir side
Like Quivers hung, and with Præamble sweet
Of charming symphonie they introduce
Thir sacred Song, and waken raptures high;
No voice exempt, no voice but well could joine
Melodious part, such concord is in Heav'n.

(*PL* III, 344-371)

It is the motion of the light in Heaven that renders it interesting;
as D. C. Allen has suggested, "It is motion in full brightness that
enlarges the extended descriptions of the epic".[7] It is the fluidity of
light that keeps God's order from dryness and coldness. In the passage from Book III, the motion is continuous, roughly concentric;
moving out and then back in warm continuity. The shout of the angels
moves out suddenly and raggedly but then returns in echo, resonantly: "Heav'n rung / With Jubilee". Significantly, the phrase
"sweet / As from blest voices, uttering joy", separates with a different
quality the consideration of resonance, sound and its echo. Immediately there follows sound in gigantic filling, outward motion:

and loud Hosanna's filld
Th' eternal Regions.

This motions turns inward in the next line:

lowly reverent
Towards either Throne they bow, and to the ground
With solemn adoration down they cast
Thir Crowns inwove with Amarant and Gold.

This is an image of order but one so alive with motion and sound as
to be radiant. One might say that motion and sound here become

[7]   Don Cameron Allen, *The Harmonious Vision* (Baltimore, 1954), p. 106.

fused into a kind of life-principle. Professor Allen analyzes the development of the imagery throughout the "tryptich" and ends with this statement of unity:

From the devout obedience of infinite number we and they [the angels] pass into the realm of an immaculate eternity so that in the end the many is received into the one, "such concord is in Heav'n".[8]

The "immaculate eternity" may suggest too much of stiffness, but Professor Allen convincingly demonstrates the fluidity and life of the heavenly unity, the capacity of the pattern to send out and reassimilate light-motion. The "lowly reverent" is magnificently qualified by the larger motions of blossoming and return and there is complex, almost tangled, luxuriant life in "resplendent locks inwreath'd with beams, / Now in loose Garlands thick thrown off".

The image of the angels ranked about God is an important one. Milton is more explicitly demonstrating the life of the image when he describes the angels after the exaltation of the Son:

> That day, as other solemn dayes, they spent
> In song and dance about the sacred Hill,
> Mystical dance, which yonder starrie Spheare
> Of Planets and of fixt in all her Wheeles
> Resembles nearest, mazes intricate,
> Eccentric, intervolv'd, yet regular
> Then most, when most irregular they seem,
> And in thir motions harmonie Divine.
>
> (*PL* V, 618-625)

Here the explicit irregularity and comparison with the stars complicate and make "living" the regularity; and of course the music adds another living perspective.

The use of surface irregularity to suggest a rich complex order has been used by Milton in several significant prose passages: in the first chapter of *The Reason for Church Government* Milton describes the complex richness of heavenly discipline:

Yet it is not to be conceiv'd that those eternall effluences of sanctity and love in the glorified Saints should by this meanes [the" golden survaying reed" of discipline] be confin'd and cloy'd with repetition of that which

---

8   *Ibid.*, p. 100.

is prescrib'd, but that our happinesse may orbe it selfe into a thousand vagancies of glory and delight, and with a kinde of eccentricall equation be as it were an invariable Planet of joy and felicity...[9]

And in the *Tetrachordon* the irregularity of heavenly motion is used to argue the need for humaneness:

For Nature hath her *Zodiac* also, keepes her great annual circuit over human things as truly as the Sun and Planets in the firmament; hath her *anomalies*, hath her obliquites in ascensions and declinations, accesses and recesses, as blamelesly as they in heaven. And sitting in her planetary Orb with two rains in each hand, one strait, the other loos, tempers the cours of minds as well as bodies to several conjunctions and oppositions, freindly, or unfreindly aspects, consenting oftest with reason, but never contrary.[10]

As early as the "Second Prolusion" Milton recognized the dryness of mere regularity:

If you rob the heavens of this music, you devote those wonderful minds and subordinate gods of yours to a life of drudgery, and condemn them to the treadmill.[11]

I do not wish to argue that Heaven is cozily human, but I think it is clear that the order of Heaven is not mechanical or cold. It is instinct with life in the marvelous and subtle use of motion-light-sound in a pattern of impregnating motion outward and return. The word *radiance* is valuable here; in its adjectival form it is concentrated in the descriptions of Heaven and its inhabitants. The word suggests, if not returning light, at least effective, continuing light.

Light is fecund in Heaven. Involved with motion and sound it impregnates, perpetuates itself, then returns to its source. Light is fluid and potent and returning. (The fountain of light is an admirable symbol here.[12]) And the great apostrophe to light in Book III is in keeping with the treatment of heavenly light throughout the poem:

> So much the rather thou Celestial light
> Shine inward, and the mind through all her powers

---

[9]   Yale *Prose*, I, 752.
[10]   Yale *Prose*, II, 680-681.
[11]   Yale *Prose*, I, 237.
[12]   As in *Paradise Regained* IV, 289.

> Irradiate, there plant eyes, all mist from thence
> Purge and disperse, that I may see and tell
> Of things invisible to mortal sight.
>
> (PL III, 51-55)

Here there is literal potency in the outward motion of light (*outward* from the source, contrapuntally *inward* to Milton) and the movement back is in the poet's heightened awareness: "That I may see and tell". This movement we must take seriously.[13]

And What Can Heav'n Shew More?

Again, in Hell, Milton provides us with a basic critical question:

> This Desart soile
> Wants not her hidden lustre, Gemms and Gold;
> Nor want we skill or Art, from whence to raise
> Magnificence; and what can Heav'n shew more?
>
> (II, 270-273)

We are compelled to answer, and in our answer must come an evaluation of the quality of a place, of the splendors of Hell. This is close to our evaluation of Satan, but I shall try to keep the two analyses separate though one should lead into the other. I should like, too, to make profitable comparison with Heaven, though there is no chronological warrant from the poem.

Hell, like Heaven, has light, motion, music – "order". But the unity in Hell is in process of dispersing, the energy is dissipating, the light is wasting. The motion of hell is out to dispersion, not out to impregnation and return. This view is I think relevant to consideration of the claim of heroic energy in Satan.

If the light of Heaven is *radiant*, the light of hell is glittery. It sparkles with a hard, sterile ferocity and falls on darkness without any afterglow or any other image of *sustained* illumination. At its best, Hell's light is continual, Heaven's is continuous. Perhaps this is as good a way as any of describing the celebrated paradoxes of Hell's lighting:

---

[13] Scholarship has, of course, taken this seriously. I do not wish to rehearse the recent finding of Miltonists on the metaphor, but to suggest one of the ways in which it operates. Professor Hughes has collected many of the comments on the source of light in his edition of *Paradise Lost*. See John Milton, *Complete Poems and Major Prose*, ed. by Merritt Y. Hughes (New York, 1957), p. 199.

on all sides round
As one great Furnace flam'd, yet from those flames
No light, but rather darkness visible.

(I, 61-63)

The horrid vale is less fiery than the burning lake, but there too
light is sterile and fitful:

The seat of desolation, voyd of light,
Save what the glimmering of these livid flames
Casts pale and dreadful.

(I, 181-183)

The kind of fragmented dispersal of light that we associate with the
words *glitter, glimmer, glister*[14] is further demonstrated, on a large
scale, in Azazel's rearing of Satan's standard:

forthwith from the glittering Staff unfurld
Th' Imperial Ensign, which full high advanc't
Shon like a Meteor streaming to the Wind
With Gemms and Golden lustre rich imblaz'd,
Seraphic arms and Trophies.

(I, 535-39)

In the description of Hell's chandeliers, the description of the
mechanics of the lighting denies the simile at the end.

from the arched roof
Pendant by suttle Magic many a row
Of Starry Lamps and blazing Cressets fed
With *Naphtha* and *Asphaltus* yeilded light
As from a sky.

(I, 726-730)

The same sterile, short-lived light is in the eyes of the fallen angels
when they receive Satan's plan for corrupting man. These eyes are
sinister, predatory in the infernal atmosphere:

The bold design
Pleas'd highly those infernal States, and joy
Sparkl'd in all thir eyes.

(II, 386-388)

And in Book X, we have a wry shrinking of Satan's light:

---

[14] But Milton does not neatly restrict them to use in Hell. His theories of good
and evil are too complicated.

> At last as from a Cloud his fulgent head
> And shape Starr bright appeer'd, or brighter, clad
> With what permissive glory since his fall
> Was left him, or false glitter.
>
> (449-52)

Hell-light is harsh, intermittent, sterile. It does not generally illuminate Hell, or provide for its own propagation. But I do not wish
to cut myself off from those moments of brightness in Hell, nor from
the test, which Professor Stein describes in his essay on Satan, of
"submitting an idea to a dramatic structure".[15] So, there is magnificence of a kind in the angels' response to Satan's call for war in
Book I.

> He spake: and to confirm his words, out-flew
> Millions of flaming swords, drawn from the thighs
> Of mighty Cherubim; the sudden blaze
> Far round illumin'd hell: highly they rag'd
> Against the Highest, and fierce with grasped Arms
> Clash'd on thir sounding Shields the din of war,
> Hurling defiance toward the Vault of Heav'n.   (I, 663-669)

Here there is brightness, and it spreads outwards. But its life-ex-
pectancy is severely qualified by the "sudden", and the brilliance
dims when we become finally aware of the perspective: the moral
perspective is established by the emphasis on height and depth
(highly ... highest) which renders the final defiance *upward* absurd.
Here the figure of the circle of energy is finally qualified by its being
placed in a vertical perspective. In the same kind of dramatic testing of qualities, Milton shows Satan leaving the council

> with pomp Supream,
> And God-like imitated State; him round
> A Globe of fierie Seraphim inclos'd
> With bright imblazonrie, and horrent Arms.   (II, 510-513)

Here, apart from the initial "editorial" tension, there is the conflict of brilliance and tightness; "inclos'd/ With bright imblazon-
rie", is over-crowded and tight in sound and meaning. The scene
reminds one of heads of state uglily hemmed in by their symbols of

---

[15] Arnold Stein, *Answerable Style* (Minneapolis, 1953), p. 3.

power, their bodyguards.[16] In general, the magnificence is radically qualified in the drama of Hell, its light and sound and motion dissipated and dispersed. The "grasped Arms/ Clash'd on thir sounding Shields the din of war" surely is loud, and it echoes; but the sound gets only about half way up and not out of the abyss.

The order of Hell is spatially defective. The horrid vale, for example, is less horrible than the burning lake, but it is slightly off-center, preparing us for the great speech of Satan's on mind and place and the substitution of self for direction. While Satan is in Hell, he is significantly the center:

> He now prepar'd
> To speak; whereat thir doubl'd Ranks they bend
> From wing to wing, and half enclose him round
> With all his Peers...   (I, 615-618)

The self becomes place and operates spatially:

> And now his heart
> Distends with pride, and hardning in his strength
> Glories...   (I, 571-573)

But often the order of the circle is qualified by the ironic perspective of height and depth:

> High on a Throne of Royal State, which far
> Outshon the wealth of *Ormus* and of *Ind*,
> Or where the gorgeous East with richest hand
> Showrs on her Kings *Barbaric* Pearl and Gold
> Satan exalted sat, by merit rais'd
> To that bad eminence.   (II, 1-6)

But Hell for the other fallen angels is horizontal and potentially a dangerous plain; Belial reminds his friends of the possibility of being

> swallowd up and lost
> In the wide womb of uncreated night.   (II, 149-150)

When the "heroic energy" of Hell goes outward it is in some danger.

And that energy does go outward; it is dispersed and dissipated. Even in the movement of the first two books, "Satan's books", the

[16] I recognize the limitations of this kind of present-day analogue, but there is a passing relevance, a minor aid to understanding the poem, in, say, the films of the Nurenberg rallies.

central energy of light-motion-sound is dissipated out toward the
dangerous edges of Hell. The angels

> Disband, and wandring, each his several way
> Pursues, as inclination or sad choice
> Leads him perplext...   (II, 523-525)

> Others more milde,
> Retreated in a silent valley, sing
> With notes Angelical...   (546-548)

The explorers set out boldly to follow the rivers but end

> Thus roving on
> In confus'd march forlorn...   (614-615)

This is a lyrical and sad dispersal, but it is dispersal, the heroic energy "peters out"; the movement is outward from force and it returns
disillusioned, hollow, like the sound of the angels hailing Mammon

> as when hollow Rocks retain
> The sound of blustring winds...   (285-286)

Song has its poignancy still and its effect, a quiet suspending of
activity, and a charming; but it follows eloquence in this landscape,
"in wandring mazes lost" (II, 561). One is reminded of the wonderful expiration of the pagan gods in the *Nativity Ode*, where we see
in contrast to the resonant music of the Word, the pagan sound re-
leased into an unresponsive landscape:

> No voice or hideous humm
>   Runs through the arched roof in words deceiving.
>
> With hollow shreik the steep of Delphos leaving.
>
> The lonely mountains o're,
> And the resounding shore,
>   A voice of weeping heard, and loud lament.
>
> In consecrated Earth
> And on the holy Hearth
>   The *Lars*, and *Lemures* moan with midnight plaint
>
> In vain the *Tyrian* Maids their wounded Thamuz mourn.
>
> In vain with Cymbals ring
>
> In vain with Timbrel'd Anthems dark
> The sable-stoled Sorcerers bear his worshipt Ark. (173-220)

But the music of the Word is somehow transitive; it has an object which it acts upon:

> When such musick sweet
> Their hearts and ears did greet,
>   As never was by mortall finger strook,
> Divinely-warbl'd voice
> Answering the stringed noise,
>   As all their souls in blissfull rapture took:
>
> Nature that heard such sound
>
>   the Airy region thrilling
>
> Ring out ye Crystall sphears,
> Once bless our humane ears.   (93-126)

The heavenly music is heard, it effects a response, it affects and in-spires. The moaning sounds of departure affect nothing, get no re-sponse, they expire; like air from a punctured balloon, they simply vanish.

And on a vaster and richer scale in *Paradise Lost* the light, sound, and *energies* of Hell expire, run out at the edges, dissipate. The sounds of Hell do not set up sympathetic vibrations, the light does not reflect backward, the energy is wasted; if it turns back on itself it will be hollowly, as a recoil of self on self and a comment on the confusion of place and self. In Heaven light radiates and irradiates, plants eyes and returns fluidly and richly to its source. Sound ech-oes resonantly, dance is richly complex. A fusion of light-motion-sound infuses, suffuses, returns and revives itself.

The decorum of Heaven and Hell argue for Milton's superb and sensitive control of tough materials. This control I find central and architectonic rather than external and manipulative. As a final de-monstration of the "large-scale" decorum I would point to the rivers of Hell; these have a center point of fusion and intensity which Milton gives us immediately:

> Four infernal Rivers that disgorge
> Into the burning Lake thir baleful streams   (575-576)

From the burning center of Hell we are led by the exploring angels outward to the very negation of rivers, ice and fire, swamps and bogs and parching air. And Lethe, again, is sinisterly off-center. The rivers in effect flow backward and disperse in their sources, though technically we are speaking of the frozen Continent beyond Lethe only. The movement, in any case, is outward and dispersed from the geographical center of Hell. The relevant comparison here is not with Heaven but Paradise where we have four other rivers:

> Southward through *Eden* went a River large,
> Nor chang'd his course, but through the shaggie hill
> Pass'd underneath ingulft, for God had thrown
> That Mountain as his Garden mould high rais'd
> Upon the rapid current, which through veins
> Of porous Earth with kindly thirst up drawn,
> Rose a fresh Fountain, and with many a rill
> Waterd the Garden; thence united fell
> Down the steep glade, and met the neather Flood,
> Which from his darksom passage now appeers
> And now divided into four main Streams,
> Runs divers, wandring many a famous Realme...
>
> (*PL* IV, 223-234)

The waterworks of the Garden have been criticized; but the answer to the criticism has been made and it is relevant here:

It is a compressed myth of natural sympathy and order, between light and darkness, between the waters below and the waters above; growing things are blessedly in the center, thirsting downward for darkness and earth and water, thirsting upward for light and sky and water.[17]

The rivers of Hell are the reverse, off-center and suicidal almost, dispersing in swamps and the frozen continent.

Hell and Heaven are "moral *arenas*, the points of relation for moral action";[18] for Milton place is "a moral dimension".[19] It is not, then, merely a matter of Hell parodying Heaven's furniture in a quest for a witty symmetry. The largest requirements of decorum – consistent unity with rich variety – are fulfilled in Milton's description of Heaven and Hell. The furniture, the landscape, the lighting and sound of Heaven is richly, resonantly unified. As *place*, Heaven is successful; it remains to examine its chief inhabitant later. Hell has been more often praised, but not perhaps for the right

[17] Stein, *op. cit.*, p. 65.
[18] Isabel Gamble MacCaffrey, *Paradise Lost as 'Myth'* (Cambridge, 1959), p. 68.
[19] *Ibid.*, p. 70.

reason. It is, I think, successfully interesting and successfully limited. The motions of expiration and dispersal dominate the place. The dissipation of heroic energy is implicit in the total picture of Hell. This brings us to Satan.

C. SATAN: FARDEST FROM HIM IS BEST

One approaches the problem of Satan with a caution bred of reading too many studies of him; that many of these studies are shrill or embarrassingly open to charges of personal aggrandizement is also sobering. I should like to examine Satan under two aspects. First, I wish to examine him as a consistent "character", a problem in *decorum personae*. This analysis I shall organize about the charge by Professor Waldock that Satan is degraded, rather than "allowed" to degenerate. Secondly, I should like to attempt to show that Satan does not violate the larger unity of the poem. He is not too big for the poem. Or, his "heroic energy" is not uncontrolled. The two tracks of analysis should not be contradictory and at times should cross or run together.

We begin the examination of Waldock's hypothesis by attending to his conception of hell with its "un-hell-like characteristic ... the atmosphere of busy planning..."[20] The legitimate Hell is swallowed up "amid the teeming interests of Books I and II..."[21] I would hope that recent analyses of hell, mine included, would qualify that statement seriously. Satan does not start out as inhabitant of a place as pleasantly busy as Professor Waldock would have us believe. Nor does he, then, start out as purely energetic on his road to being manipulated. Waldock's main attack is on the suddenness and arbitrariness of changes in Satan's character. His initial overestimation of Satan is one source of his misunderstanding of the progress of this character.

Here I wish to engage the charge that Milton "degrades" Satan. Professor Waldock argues that the character himself is not richly and continuously developed from his first appearance, but rather in

[20] Waldock, *op. cit.*, p. 94.
[21] *Ibid.*, p. 93.

a series of arbitrarily connected emblems. "Perhaps", Professor Waldock hedges, "Satan never was a character in the full sense of the word".[22] But the main charge is against the arbitrariness of changes:

It is a pretended exhibition of changes occurring; actually it is of the nature of an assertion that certain changes occur. The changes do not generate themselves from within: they are imposed from without. Satan, in short, does not degenerate: *he is degraded.*[23]

The critical problem here is to examine the character where he changes or is about to change and determine whether that transition is dramatic and consistent with the character or imposed and inconsistent.[24] I shall follow Waldock, but not strictly, in considering "the main stages in Satan's downward course",[25] chronologically after the War in Heaven.

The complexity of Satan and the extent to which our knowledge of the character *grows* even in Book I is attested by the fact that we accept the opening of Book II, with its scintillating paradox:

> Satan exalted sat, by merit rais'd
> To that bad eminence.   (5-6)

We accept without complaint the double perspective on Satan, the pomp and pomposity at once, as a just culmination of the facts of Hell we have already experienced. And we continue to experience this double perspective throughout the Council in Hell. It is here that Professor Waldock registers a strong complaint.

As the climax of the Council in Hell, Satan accepts the task of corrupting man to spite God. He accepts the task alone and we are given to understand that his insisting on doing the task alone is a pointed demonstration of unheroic vanity:

> Thus saying rose
> The Monarch, and prevented all reply,
> Prudent, least from his resolution rais'd
> Others among the chief might offer now

---

[22] *Ibid.*, p. 86.

[23] *Ibid.*, p. 83.

[24] Of course the critical terminology is fuzzy here. What character in literature isn't "manipulated" by the author? I take it Waldock means here *decorum personae.*

[25] Waldock, *op. cit.*, p. 83.

> (Certain to be refus'd) what erst they feard;
> And so refus'd might in opinion stand
> His Rivals, winning cheap the high repute
> Which he through hazard huge must earn.   (II, 466-473)

The passage has been criticized for editorializing Satan's courage; the drama asserts Satan's courage, the stage directions deny it.[26] Apart from the exquisite tact of the editorial itself, the drama prepares us for this exposition of Satan's motives. Satan's great speech, "O Progeny of Heav'n, Empyreal Thrones" (430-466) is pronounced while he is seated, "unmov'd thus spake" (429). It is Satan's own timing that emphasizes his last spoken line:

> this enterprize
> None shall partake with me. Thus saying rose
> The Monarch...   (465-467)

The movement is dramatic, not editorial, emphasis, though it moves eloquently *into* editorial emphasis. The real gesture of separation is greater than the gesture of "sacrifice". In the editorial comment the separateness is maintained in the reference to Satan as "*Monarch*" (always used by Milton in the poem with full etymological weight). The movement from "Prudent" to "Rivals" to "Forbidding" is less sensitive, but the dramatic work has been done. Satan then separates himself in his speech as well as in gesture; apart from the overt melodramatic emphasis on the difficulties of trip, there is the careful emphasis on specialization:

> intend at home,
> While here shall be our home, what best may ease
> The present misery, and render Hell
> More tollerable; if there be cure or charm
> To respite or deceive, or slack the pain
> Of this ill Mansion: intermit no watch
> Against a wakeful Foe, while I abroad
> Through all the Coasts of dark destruction seek
> Deliverance for us all.   (457-465)

I am not concerned with Satan's arrogance here. I want to emphasize his dramatic isolation of self, even from his followers, before, and consistent with, the editorial identification of separation. The

---

[26] Waldock, *op. cit.*, p. 80.

tact of the scene I find extraordinary, dramatically smooth and "fair" to Satan, and completely assured. The relation between Satan and his followers is beautifully elaborated and muted in the poignant image of the setting sun, but the isolation of Satan has been established in consistent dramatic terms.

Satan's acceptance of the mission to earth can be well compared to Christ's acceptance of a mission to earth. Satan's acceptance ends with an isolation from others, a retreat, as it were, into "pure" self. Christ's great speech beginning "Father, thy word is past, man shall find grace" (III, 227) ends with the return to heart of light.

> Then with the multitude of my redeemd
> Shall enter Heaven long absent, and returne,
> Father, to see thy face, wherein no cloud
> Of anger shall remain, but peace assur'd,
> And reconcilement; wrauth shall be no more
> Thenceforth, but in thy presence Joy entire.   (260-265)

The two motions,[27] one of isolation, one of return, are consistent with the views I have presented of Hell and Heaven. But my point about Satan here is that his isolation develops internally at this point of transition and is not imposed.[28]

In the encounter with Sin and Death at the outset of his journey, Satan is arrogant, brave, cunning, and eminently adaptable in his rhetoric and external "feelings". These aspects of him, we have seen earlier. Perhaps of most interest is the fact of Satan's adaptability. In Hell he adapts to the needs of his followers, at Hell gates he adapts to the need of his sinful past's pressure on the present and vice versa. From "I know thee not, nor ever saw till now/ Sight more detestable then him and thee" (II, 744-745), Satan moves to "Dear Daughter... And my fair Son here" (817-818). The point has not been overlooked. I use it simply to show Satan repeating a suppression of emotions, but more elaborately, more obviously near

[27] In comparing these two scenes, Joseph Summers contrasts the proud "I" of Satan's speech with the humble and loving "me" of Christ's speech. "The question in Heaven is not 'whom shall we find / Sufficient', but 'where shall we find such love'" (*The Muses Method*, Cambridge, 1962, pp. 179-180).

[28] In a way William Empson is with me here, when he defends Satan's prearrangements with Beelzebub. He is arguing for the sense of the scene. See William Empson, "The Satan of Milton", *Hudson Review*, XII (Spring, 1960), 45.

disguise. This is a sign of Satan's degeneration; the process is too subtle to be a *grade* below his earlier act. It is part of the continuous process down to external adaptability, to be carried to comic and horrid extremes, which results from internal rigidity, the stony isolation of "Myself am Hell". It is a fascinating paradox of the Satanic personality, but one of which we have been aware from the opening scenes in Hell, with Satan in "the trap of leadership".[29]

The tension of external adaptability with internal rigidity is echoed in the increasing psychological tension and physical control which results in recklessness, hysteria. As Satan increases the pressure on his emotions, the closer these emotions come to bursting through. So, near the end of Book II, "*Satan* staid not to reply" to Chaos (1010). But here he still is proceeding with some of the dark stateliness of the beginning of his journey:

> and now with ease
> Wafts on the calmer wave by dubious light.
>
> (II, 1041-1042)

His shrouds and tackle may be torn, but there is a superb and sinister ease in

> Weighs his spread wings, at leasure to behold
> Farr off th' Empyreal Heav'n...   (1046-1047)

In Book III, the verbs change. Satan:

> throws
> His flight precipitant, and windes with ease
> Through the pure marble Air...   (562-564)

Satan has not always controlled his trajectory, but here the throwing is his own doing, as it is, with more assurance, at the end of Book III where he

> Throws his steep flight in many an Aerie wheele
> Nor staid, till on *Niphates* top he lights.   (741-742)

Satan's next adaptation to circumstance is disguise and once more we feel the tightening, one more turn of the screw of self. (Admittedly this is "stage" but one prepared for, smoothly anticipated):

[29]   Stein, *op. cit.*, p. 10. Roland M. Frye writes "Having abandoned his true being, Satan becomes the continuous poseur, forever striking attitudes and pretentious postures" (*op. cit.*, p. 36).

> And now a stripling Cherube he appeers,
> Not of the prime, yet such as in his face
> Youth smil'd Celestial, and to every Limb
> Sutable grace diffus'd, so well he feignd;
> Under a Coronet his flowing haire
> In curles on either cheek plaid, wings he wore
> Of many a colourd plume sprinkl'd with Gold,
> His habit fit for speed succinct, and held
> Before his decent steps a Silver wand.   (III, 636-644)

The "tinsel Theatricality"[30] is here quite overt; Satan's internal pride has forced him into a kind of external humiliation. He is forced to disguise himself, and the taste of his disguise here is to be measured by comparing this cherub with Raphael or with Adam. (In addition Milton is, I think, having a delicious little joke on decency, even twenty-five years later. This is developed in the comment on Hypocrisie in lines 681-688.) In any case, Satan's habit of dissembling has now developed into the practice of disguise. Even to those who find Satan's dissembling in Hell admirable, that dissembling must appear transformed into the technique of disguise through a continuum of dramatic stress and change rather than from external "manipulation". The creature in disguise is potential in the heroic dissembler.

We are now on Mt. Niphates. Satan is in full light. He is away from the followers to whom he is "bound". He is at an advanced stage of the decay of the whole self (internal and external) which results from the worship of the self isolated from God. And he is psychologically wound too tightly. All the subterranean complexities of Satan erupt into a confession that strikes us as simple and ingenuous:

> Which way I flie is Hell; my self am Hell;
>   is there no place
> Left for Repentance, none for Pardon left?
> None left but by submission; and that word
> *Disdain* forbids me, and my dread of shame
> Among the spirits beneath, whom I seduc'd...
>   (IV, 75, 79-83)

The confession itself does not act as a cathartic of evil; it is, in a sense, like the public confessions of our time, a simple expression

30   The phrase is John Peter's, *op. cit.*, p. 51.

of the internal evil[31] (and I am not speaking of the "insincere" confession). In this sense it is allied to the simple signs of Satan's degeneracy to follow: the fall to cormorant-toad-snake. The fall is fast, but it is continuous and it is the fall of a single character. A cardboard stunt man is not substituted suddenly at the beginning of Book IV. Disguise, and its implications about the sacrifice of total self, is implicit in the Satan of Books I and II and subtly developed and enlarged throughout the poem until the last climactic transformation of Book X.

The process of disguise is itself "outward", that is, it represents a physical retreat from the reality and energy of the center. The heroic voyage of Satan which starts firmly is resolutely ambiguous in its relation to centers. As a trip out from Hell it *is* heroic, especially compared with the motions of dispersal of the other fallen angels in Book II. That is "the dramatic role of evil", but as that heroic voyage proceeds, it changes. It loses its stature as willed journey in the change of kind of movement. At the same time it becomes more virulent. By the time it organizes itself in relation to Paradise it becomes a journey of violation. This is clearly seen in the leaping of the walls of Paradise:

> Due entrance he disdaind, and in contempt
> At one slight bound high over leap'd all bound
> Of Hill or highest Wall, and sheer within
> Lights on his feet. As when a prowling Wolfe...
>
> (IV,180-183)

And Milton launches into another Wolf-in-the-fold simile, which is customarily used by him to present the violation of a sacred place of the spirit.[32] Satan's energies here are virulent, but not heroic; the virulence of Satan's motion here will give way to the subtlety of his persuasion. Neither operation of his character is purely or

---

[31]   Confession operates this way, even "sincere" confession, as our age can testify. The great public political confessions of the past thirty years have taught us to suspend our disbelief. The skepticism roused by the Moscow trials of 1938 has been I think replaced with an uneasy kind of belief in them. I recognize that I speak of public confession and that Satan is now alone; but the relation between complex inverted motivation and simple overt expression still holds.
[32]   See for example "Lycidas", 1. 128 and *PL* XII, 508, and among numerous instances in the prose, Columbia *Milton*, V, 58 and IX, 147.

even largely heroic. The great journey from Hell is the closest thing to heroism and its termini affect our view of it.

I insert here, following the order of the poem, an unchronological comment. William Empson has given considerable attention to Satan's Conclave in Heaven by way of making his claim for the rationale of rebellion. There has been intellectual discussion, and Satan is thus no fly-by-night sophist;

> Milton (being so learned a man) would not seriously despise Satan for disbelieving his creation; nor should we read that into the poem, because Satan is not meant to become contemptible till his character collapses after he has doubted his own thesis upon Niphates top.[33]

But the whole of the Satanic conclave in Heaven is touched with a sinister comedy which culminates in the War. And the opening dramatic statement of Satan's role in the revolt seems to me to set the tone:

> Contemptuous, and his next subordinate
> Awak'ning, thus to him in secret spake.
> Sleepst thou Companion dear, what sleep can close
> Thy eye-lids?   (V, 671-674)

The decorum of Heaven can sustain no whispers especially when they remind us of the evil toad in the ears of innocence in Book IV which we have already seen. This is not chronological evidence we bring to bear, but it most surely suffuses our apprehension of the scene. This is no purely heroic conspiracy.

Satan's heroic energy is our concern now. And throughout he is shown in the process of de-energizing, largely in terms of his relation to the center. After tempting Eve

> Back to the Thicket slunk
> The guiltie Serpent...   (IX, 784-785)

But the great dispersal comes in Book X when Satan returns with the good news, stagily sneaks into the center of Hell[34] and makes his announcement jauntily, ending

> What remains, ye Gods,
> But up and enter now into full bliss.   (X, 502-503)

[33] Empson, *op. cit.*, p. 58.
[34] Professor Stein points out "the histrionic mounting of the throne incognito" *op. cit.*, p. 8.

Instead of bliss, they enter hiss (a not unintended play on words). Satan falls outward and down and the scene becomes one gigantic *exit* from the center of Hell. The devils all flow in wriggling horizontal lines away from the center. Far from being simple (Professor Waldock's comic cartoon surely implies one emblematic pratfall, no dynamic handling of complexities) this scene presents a remarkable handling of vistas. We move out beyond Satan, with the lesser devils in anticipation looking toward the gates of Pandemonium, "Sublime with expectation", (536) for Satan. Then we see the "crowd / Of ugly Serpents" and

> horror on them fell,
> And horrid sympathie. (539-540)

This time we're trampled by these new snakes, with whom we were just standing, as they move with the larger serpents outward and away. The final vista is of the false tree, blatantly unreal and false, desperately away from the center of physical, psychological and aesthetic reality.

Throughout the scene we have the celebrated hissing, "the finest sibilant music in the language".[35] It operates as more than decor:

> Thus was th' applause they meant,
> Turnd to exploding hiss, triumph to shame
> Cast on themselves from thir own mouths. (545-547)

This sound has a tangible quality; it really escapes outward, disperses, expires, and, like vomit, befouls.

The hissing sound of expiration is so firmly used that one is tempted to relate it to early mentions of Satan and his friends as filled with air:

> And now his heart
> Distends... (I, 571-572)

> So spake the grieslie terrour, and in shape,
> So speaking and so threatning, grew tenfold
> More dreadful and deform: on th' other side
> Incenst with indignation *Satan* stood... (II, 704-707)

> On th' other side *Satan* allarm'd
> Collecting all his might dilated stood,
> Like *Teneriff* or *Atlas* unremov'd. (IV, 985-987)

---

[35] Edith Sitwell quoted in Hughes' edition of *Paradise Lost, op. cit.*, p. 419.

I have suggested that the flight of pagan Gods in the "Nativity Ode" resembles expiration, air from a punctured balloon. And in this final scene in Hell, the hissing suggests the same. Milton had no experience with flat-tires, and I do not wish to push the point unduly. But something of the strategy I describe he might have remembered in Spenser's treatment of Orgoglio:

> But soone as breath out of his brest did pas,
> That huge great body, which the gyaunt bore,
> Was vanisht quite, and of that monstrous mas
> Was nothing left, but like an emptie bladder was.
>
> (*FQ* I, VIII, 24)

Or we might remember Milton's use of the Antaeus simile in *Paradise Regained*:

> Throttl'd at length in the Air, expir'd and fell   (*PR* IV, 568)

Closer and more suggestive is Raphael's admonition on knowledge which provides an adumbration of the scene in Book X:

> Knowledge is as food, and needs no less
> Her Temperance over Appetite, to know
> In measure what the mind may well contain,
> Oppresses else with Surfet, and soon turns
> Wisdom to folly, as Nourishment to Winde.   (VII, 126-130)

The scene in *Paradise Lost* is not merely a punctured balloon any more than it is a "cartoon". It is a complex depiction of the terminus of several important themes in the portrayal of Satan and patterns crucial to the poem. The theme of dissembling and disguise reaches its climax here. The theme of the whole self and the outsider culminates here. The pattern of the center as a source of energy and renewal is summarized here for Satan in the creation of a false center, and in the dispersal and dissipation of the energies of sound and motion.

Professor Waldock's unfairness to the final scene in Hell, his insistence on the simple emblematic degradation of the villain, is symptomatic of his whole reading of Satan. Waldock refuses to read continuously and with anything like sympathy for the subtle qualifications of character. Without our awareness of the ironic perspective on Satan, the extraordinary riches of poetic perspective, Satan does emerge as a black and white character, editorialized into conformity with the gross intentions of the epic. Perhaps this is close to what Bernard Bergonzi means when he speaks of Waldock's insistence on "reading *Paradise Lost* as a simple naturalistic narrative".[36] For surely it is not that Satan is too unsubtle for one trained in the glories of modern fiction; it is that Professor Waldock reads with an eye that misses the subtleties of this verse, because, like Mr. Peter above, he isolates character from its context as a discrete continuum of modern "psychological" observations. The poem is a poem, not a collecion of scenes with bridges. Satan is not only a character with big scenes but a dramatic continuum within and consistent with the larger continuum of the poem. Milton has suceeded superbly, I think, in making Satan alive and consistent as a character throughout; just as surely he has succeeded in showing his character cut off from the source of revival, stubbornly opposed to the source of energy, and hence decreasing in stature throughout the poem.

I have been concerned here with a partial though I hope not "limited" reading of Satan. I have not undertaken to discuss fully some of the major aspects of Satan, especially where I have felt that these have been authoritatively "answered" for our time. Nor have I undertaken to answer questions which strike me as unimportant. Chiefly I am concerned with the consistency of Satan's fall and with the ways Milton keeps Satan within the poem. The latter examination revolves around the phrase propounded by Professor Tillyard:

The character of Satan expresses, as no other character or act or feature of the poem does, something in which Milton believed very strongly: heroic energy.[37]

Milton's Satan is a consistently developed figure of decreasing energy. He helps us to know God, through a series of marvelously engineered inversions. But Satan is defined, too, by the very immutability and pure rational assertiveness of God.

---

[36] Bernard Bergonzi, "Criticism and the Milton Controversy", in *The Living Milton*, ed. Frank Kermode (London, 1960), p. 179.
[37] E. M. W. Tillyard, *Milton* (London, 1930), p. 277.

D. GOD: WHO CAN EXTENUATE THEE?

Unlike Satan, He does not change as the occasion demands. He is not adaptable to person, place, or thing. He is not answerable to the exigencies of His fate. Satan adapts himself, to Sin and Death, to Eve, to his followers, to everyone but God; in this paradoxical worship of self he arrives at something not-self; he becomes virtually a technique of relativism. God is immutable.

It is characteristic of Milton's kind of honesty in the poem that he will not deaden the fundamental issues. When he set out to justify the ways of God he did not set out to palliate the ways of God, to make them easy to take. Dante's circles of light are, after all, since they symbolize the aspects of God easily acceptable to humans, more humane than Milton's school divine. It is a misrepresentation to accuse Milton's God of being too human; the accusers are supressing the desire for a *humane* God, a God of warmth, power, sympathy – whether anthropomorphic or not. Milton's God is unique, rational, and doubly assertive.

The early vision has been revised but not renounced. In *The Reason of Church-government* Milton had set forth his program:

To celebrate in glorious and lofty Hymns the throne and equipage of Gods Almightinesse, and what he works, and what he suffers to be wrought with high providence in his Church... whatsoever in religion is holy and sublime, in vertu amiable, or grave, whatsoever hath passion or admiration in all the changes of that which is call'd fortune from without, or the wily suttleties and refluxes of mans thoughts from within, all these things with a solid and treatable smoothnesse to paint out and describe.[38]

The fervor of this passage is missing from the speeches of God the Father, though not from those of Christ. Surely, however, "the solid and treatable smoothnesse" is there, as recent criticism has demonstrated. Truth is not necessarily pleasant in all its parts, and Milton insists on the Fall as center to his poem; his use of the rhetorical schemes suggests artistic emphasis, not neurotic indulgence.

To consider Milton's God is to consider God and surely this is one reason why the study and teaching of Milton is steadily exciting. In a study of decorum, one can only attend to partial aspects, here

[38]   Yale *Prose*, I, 817.

three matters of special interest. The first is that God escapes the requirements of *decorum personae* by not being a person. God is God: His only referent is His self. The source of all hierarchy, energy, order cannot Himself be described in terms of hierarchy, energy, order. He is eminently not human; hence sympathy in its root and profound sense is impossible.

The assertion that Man will be saved through divine grace and not his own will, for example, however true, can only smack of self-aggrandizement when it is made by God himself. (174-178)[39]

God is criticized for being egocentric, (but it is hard to know why God shouldn't be, since He is *the* center) and self-aggrandizing. This would be indecorous in a good father, a good king, a good man, or for that matter, a good angel. God the Father is outside of category. Irene Samuel has put the matter efficiently:

What we learn, to begin with, is that, unfortunately for Satan, the God of *Paradise Lost* is not merely another being on whose pattern he can model his rebel state, but Total Being, *the* Primal Energy, *the* Voice of Reason, *the* Moral Law that makes possible a physical cosmos. He is *the* Creator ... *the* Intelligence ... To try to read the dialogue that follows (III, 77) without allowing the first speaker his full nature would indeed make nonsense of the scene.[40]

The decorum of this scene, the use of character which makes part of the larger unity of the poem, is the result of an escape from the decorum of humanity. Milton insists on the non-human, non-answerable aspects of God the Father.

Miss Samuel then leads us into the second important point for our consideration:

The flat statement of fact, past, present, and future, the calm analyses and judgment of deeds and principles – these naturally strike the ear that has heard Satan's ringing utterance as cold and impersonal. They should. For the omniscient voice of the omnipotent moral law speaks simply what is. Here is no orator using rhetoric to persuade, but the nature of things expanding itself in order to present fact and principle unadorned.[41]

It is not miscalculated frigidity that makes the words of God terri-

---

[39] Peter, *op. cit.*, p. 13.
[40] Irene Samuel, "The Dialogue in Heaven; A Reconsideration of *Paradise Lost* III _ _ _ I _ 417", *PMLA*, LXXII (Sept. 1957), 602-603.
[41] *Ibid.*

ble, separate, immutable and unanswerable to the decorum of hu-
man-kind. J.B. Broadbent has expanded Miss Samuel's treatment
by showing us that a God not susceptible to metaphor is treated in
extraordinarily complex rhetorical terms. Mr. Broadbent points out
"the peculiarly prosodic and verbal kind of rhetoric" that is heavily
concentrated in Books III and IX, then continues:

The monopoly of Books III and IX indicates that iterative and verbal
figures belong especially to theological contexts. In both books the theology is presented in the form of debate. The debate in Heaven is often
linked with that in Pandemonium; but the devils' debate is much more
forensic. They apply the rules of disposition and suasion, but their
arguments are urging of individual ambitions, manifest in language, which
is more tropal than schematic. In contrast, the debates in Books III and
IX are dialectical. This universalizes the heavenly debates and gives them
something of the character of interior monologues, unifying the persons
of the Godhead and internalizing the relations between Satan as tempter,
Adam, and Eve. These theological contexts are bare of tropes; so we
have an essentially abstract and verbal treatment of the poem's central
issues.[42]

Mr. Broadbent is well aware of the critical question here, and I
think he is correct in his conclusions:

Can issues presented so formally take effect in a poem which elsewhere
appeals strongly to the senses and imagination? Blake's answer would be
No: schematic rhetoric is only symptom of the tyranny of a life-denying
rationality over the fluid and passionate nature of language. A less
ethnocentric answer is that Milton was justified historically, as well as
temperamentally, in worshipping the kind of rationality celebrated in
Paradise Lost; that he was justified artistically in using a rational poetic
to construct a theodicy with; and that we can learn from this.[43]

Historically and artistically as well as temperamentally, Milton's
rational poetic is justifiable.

Professor Broadbent's analysis is surely more relevant and accurate than that of Malcolm Ross. Ross attacks Milton's imagery,
the symbolism of Heaven and God as "evidence of a vicarious exultation in sheer power"; "Milton's despotic God is the sick man's
dream of strength, the poetic sublimation of anger, frustration and

[42] J. B. Broadbent, "Milton's Rhetoric", *Modern Philology*, LVI (May, 1959),
230.
[43] *Ibid.*, p. 233.

vengeance".[44] Ross's conclusion is intimately related to the problem of decorum:

The validity of symbols with social reference is determined by society, and not by the genius of the individual, however great that genius be... The artist is a social animal.[45]

The concern is for the decorum of words, not the decorum of words in context. The use of gold in Hell does not render gold evil, nor does the energy of Satan taint the energy of God. The symbol with social reference is not imported dead and unchanged into the context of the poem. The poem, the parts of the poem in fact, modify *gold* and *energy* in context, as the context of Milton's prose modified the symbols of Anglicanism. Mr. Ross insists on the life of the word and its modification by usage up to the time of its participation in the poem. This is to treat the poem as a sepulchre for words, instead of as a place where words have their very highest order of life. I would hope that the preceding chapters obviate the impression that I am arguing for the complete autonomy of the poem.

The observations on style by Miss Samuel and Mr. Broadbent are illumined by the tradition of language in accordance with the subject (πρὸς τὰ πράγματα), the simple style of which Aristotle speaks when he says, "Nobody uses fine language when teaching geometry".[46] The tradition of simplicity for speaking of difficult truth Augustine propounded in a very practical way:

The subdued style has its own proper functions. It answers very difficult questions and proves them with an unexpected explanation.[47]

The whole Stoic ideal of rhetoric and behind that the Platonic and Aristotelian ideal of language as a transparent medium of thought may operate here also. God is addressing the Son: What adjustments are necessary for the audience? We can remember Milton himself on the language of truth: "The very essence of Truth is

[44] Malcolm M. Ross, *Milton's Royalism* (Ithaca, 1943), pp. 92, 100.
[45] *Ibid.*, p. 147.
[46] Aristotle, *Rhetoric*, transl. by W. Rhys Roberts, in *The Rhetoric and The Poetics of Aristotle*, ed. by Friedrich Solmsen (New York, 1954), p. 166.
[47] St. Augustine, *Christian Instruction*, in *The Fathers of the Church*, II (New York, 1947), 227-228.

plainnesse and brightnes; the darknes and crookednesse is our own".[48]

   After insisting upon the uniqueness and un-sympathy and the rational assertiveness of God the Father, Milton will portray Christ. And this is the third important point. God is in fact a kind of antiphon. The opening scene in Heaven carefully moves from God's opening statement of Justice through his transitional last lines on Mercy. Christ almost literally echoes and contextually expands that Mercy in his speech:

> O Father, gracious was that word which clos'd
> Thy sovran sentence, that Man should find grace;
> For which both Heav'n and Earth shall high extoll
> Thy praises, with th' innumerable sound
> Of Hymns and sacred Songs, wherewith thy Throne
> Encompass'd shall resound thee ever blest.   (144-149)

God's next speech, though softening as it relates to Christ, retains its stiff rationality:

> This my long sufferance and my day of grace
> They who neglect and scorn, shall never taste;
> But hard be hard'nd, blind be blinded more,
> That they may stumble on, and deeper fall;
> And none but such from mercy I exclude.   (198-202)

The muteness of the Heavenly Choir is followed by Christ's lovely speech of sacrifice:

> Behold mee then, mee for him, life for life
> I offer, on mee let thine anger fall;
> Account mee man; I for his sake will leave
> Thy bosom...   (236-239)

This scene with its balancing speeches of aspects of deity and its choral interludes and finale is both magnificent and moving. Again and again in the poem, Christ will echo the divine justice in some human way. In Book V Christ translates that divine justice into laughter; in Book VI, into destructive power; in Book VII, into creative love:

> So spake th'Almightie, and to what he spake
> His Word, the filial Godhead, gave effect.   (174-175)

[48]   Yale *Prose*, I, 566.

There is a non-metaphorical God and we must be aware of Him; Christ is a metaphor, a final accommodation, "the ultimate terminus of the Christian symbols".[49] And the closeness of the two expressions of deity is such as to make dramatically meaningful the paradox of the Father and the Son, or, for an anti-Trinitarian, of a God of Justice and Love.

Milton, then, is conscious of the austerity and "inhumanity" of his God and assumes that his reader will be. The purity of his image of God requires the kind of rhetorical isolation, the dialectic and schematic movement of language, which strikes the reader as barer than mere simplicity. The image of God the Father is qualified by the image of his Son. They are presented with full identities and yet in essential conjunction. The source of the paradoxes implicit in these points are doctrinal not poetic, but the poetry has here not surrendered itself to simple statement of doctrine.

This is the charge of many critics, that Milton has created difficulties for his poem by a simple-minded insistence on the doctrinal:

It is hard not to feel some slight impatience with a poet who prefers to double the intrinsic difficulties: who, not content with a God who *must*, however matters are contrived, appear somewhat vindictive, goes out of his way to convict him on his very first appearance of flagrant disingenuousness and hypocrisy ... The human impression is what is important.[50]

I tack on the last sentence because it is a key to Professor Waldock's position, and to that of Mr. Peter who bears burden to this popular song:

Thus Theology's demand for a clearness at the outset about Man's Free Will and Poetry's demand for a characterization of God that will support our love and reverence cannot on Milton's terms be reconciled.[51]

Milton would reject "Poetry's demand", at least as it is put here. He would reject Poetry's right to make the demand. But then he would reject it on poetic as well as dogmatic grounds. The decorum of *this poem* modifies the kind of demands abstract Poetry (what is it?) can make on the decorum of a character.

---

[49] Frye, *God, Man and Satan*, p. 13. Mr. Frye's valuable discussion of "accommodation" is immediately relevant.
[50] Waldock, *op. cit.*, pp. 101, 102.
[51] Peter, *op. cit.*, p. 18.

"The human impression is what is important" – but not in the sense Professor Waldock insists on. And it is a matter of decorum, of what the standard for *human* is to be. Is this human decorum the twentieth century one which rejects the concept of deity or at least the possibility of its expression in other than warm, fathering terms? I suggest that Waldock, Peter, and Mr. Empson are insisting on a *decorum personae* for God that is as rigid as Thomas Rymer's for *Othello* and as limited in its regard for the poem as an organism. Empson's God is answerable to Empson's man; satisfactions Empson demands from Milton's God are based on a conception of human nature which omits God from that nature, not the *manhood in Grace* which Milton insists on everywhere in his work. To impart a modern decorum for God's performance into the reading of the poem is an act of critical irresponsibility, especially since the human nature which serves to create that decorum has changed radically during the time since Milton. What "feels right" for Mr. Empson is not finally what feels right for Milton or indeed for many twentieth century readers.[52]

It is just possible that the effort to read the poem in a context near the one which Milton wrote will enable us to be better people. In any case, it will make us better readers if we remember that decorum is not externally and rigidly imposed, that the decorum of this poem is created partially and dramatically within this poem. Professor Stein has provided an enormously stimulating clue: "Milton's style is also answerable to the as yet *unattempted*, to the poem this proves to be".[53]

God the Father is just, God the Son is loving. The Arianism of the *De Doctrina* is here genuinely subordinated. The figure of God in *Paradise Lost* is answerable to the complex doctrinal requirements of Milton's time, not ours, to the point of severe, comprehensive but not complete justification of the ways of God to man. But most especially Milton's God answers the demands of the great Christian epic which the Christian God of Justice and Love in-

[52]   William Empson, *Milton's God* (London, 1961). I am not "engaging" Mr. Empson's powerful and disturbing book, but I do think it important to label his decorum for God and man in *Paradise Lost* as simply mistaken as John Peter's.
[53]   Stein, *op. cit.*, p. 122.

spired. Justice is not always pleasant. The religious experience is not always euphoric. Fallen man is *fallen* and *man*, and man is something more than rational beast. Milton engages these facts in his treatment of God. The heaven of *Paradise Lost* does not blind with glory, despite its radiance and its dark with excessive bright. If Milton assumes that man is not the measure of God, he still takes us into a heaven to look at God with what is finally the most human and humble weakness – the desire to understand fully. One does not surrender his rationality to God; that is too easy. One uses reason with a *ruthless* honesty, though not a trivial one, as Raphael warns; and *ruthless* honesty is not inconsistent with humility. It is only the kind of honesty that wants praise for its brave fellow-ness that smacks of pride. One does not sacrifice one's self to God easily, or because one is incomplete. The Christian who is "a lively sacrifice of praise and thanksgiving"[54] will be rational and aware in his humility.

Milton recognized the problems of his God as character in a poem. He attended to them with rhetorical and dramatic skill, while refusing to ignore the strictness of God's justice. Justice and mercy are decorously treated in the poem; they are concepts to be observed operating dramatically in a context of amazing complexities. We can not cut through the complexities with the single sword of a modern decorum – the modern decorum of the human animal.

E. ADAM AND EVE IN THE GARDEN:
A HAPPY RURAL SEAT OF VARIOUS VIEW

Milton approaches the garden last of his three moral arenas or places, *topoi* in the basic Aristotelian sense. He has started at the edges of the known universe and worked *in* to the Garden. The mythic sense is generally Ptolemaic, one assumes; in any case the working spatialization of the poem creates a pronounced sense of "arrival" when the poem reaches Paradise. The mythic qualities of the Garden have been described and denied and described again,

[54] Yale *Prose*, II, 259.

until now they form, I think, one of the stable cores of thinking about the poem. I should like to touch only briefly on the mythic and then move on to Adam and Eve as decorous and supple inhabitants of the "happy rural seat of various view".

There is an extraordinary exercise of "practical" myth in creating the immediate perspective for the first sight of Adam and Eve. The sensuousness is super-biological, a tightening of the richness of God's gifts which separates the pre-lapsarian garden from gardens. But biology glimmers through in "Grazing the tender herb" or in the lovely reminiscence of Proserpina: "Her self a fairer Floure by gloomie *Dis/* Was gatherd, which cost *Ceres* all that pain" (IV, 270-271). This is the most broadly relevant of the classical allusions, but all of them contribute to the perspective of richness *and* distance from which the reader first views the couple. And the last-minute reminder of Satan's framing eye contributes further to the objectifying of our first view of our first parents:

> where the Fiend
> Saw undelighted all delight, all kind
> Of living Creatures new to sight and strange:
> Two of far nobler shape erect and tall,
> Godlike erect, with native Honour clad
> In naked Majestie seemd Lords of all,
> And worthie seemd...   (285-291)

Our vision of them ends after explicit confrontation of their inequality and their sexuality. They pass on in profile and in the distance, moving across the top part of the picture[55] so to speak, with the vivid, unliteral precision of dream. In the first view of the (mythic) Garden, the characters are mythically grand in stature and movement.

When Milton moves to the subject of pre-lapsarian love and marriage, the characters and landscape adjust delicately. The sensuousness turns warmer. Within the ring of danger from Satan's predatory rage, Adam advises Eve, and hears the story of her creation. Then the classically sensuous scene of their embrace,

> with eyes
> Of conjugal attraction unreprov'd,

[55]   The phrase is suggested by David Daiches, *Milton* (London, 1957), p. 188.

> And meek surrender, half imbracing leand
> On our first Father, half her swelling Breast
> Naked met his under the flowing Gold
> Of her loose tresses hid: he in delight
> Both of her Beauty and submissive Charms
> Smil'd with superior Love, as *Jupiter*
> On *Juno* smiles, when he impregns the Clouds
> That shed *May* Flowers; and press'd her Matron lip
> With kisses pure: aside the Devil turnd
> For envie, yet with jealous leer maligne
> Ey'd them askance...   (492-504)

Milton's Adam and Eve are completely achieved but their virtues are here almost completely potential. There is the possibility of corruption of female "shame" or to use Milton's terms of "coy submission, modest pride, / And sweet reluctant amorous delay" (310-311). But within the limits of moral order and hierarchy, the body's own sense of drama is pure.

It is the hierarchical conception of married love which Milton proceeds to develop delightfully. The relationship of man and woman is intense and private yet reflected in the Garden. With the insistence on hierarchy as an expression of God's plan, there is the idea of intimacy, of private property really, with its intensities:

> Haile wedded Love, mysterious Law, true source
> Of human ofspring, sole proprietie,
> In Paradise of all things common else.   (IV, 750-752)

The most interesting thing here is the "sole propriety"[56] which puts a daring value on the "Rites/ Mysterious of connubial Love" (742-743). The cherished, almost secret, human identity is pronounced throughout this section on the blissful bower:

> other Creature here
> Beast, Bird, Insect, or Worm durst enter none;
> Such was thir awe of Man.   (703-705)

This is God's hierarchy, the awe of our first parents in a place furnished by God; but it combines with a moving sense of the couple, their privacy, and the individual identities behind their union. How

[56] Professor William Haller has pointed out the Puritan attitude, *amour bourgeois*, as a clear challenge to *amour courtois*. See his "Hail Wedded Love", *ELH*, XIII (1946), 81-82.

completely *identified* they are we see at the close of the passage where they

> lulld by Nightingales imbraceing slept,
> And on thir naked limbs the flourie roof
> Showrd Roses, which the Morn repair'd. Sleep on
> Blest pair...   (771-774)

This is formal and archetypal; but locked tightly within the embrace is a feeling for the rich private self.

The scene expands outward with some geometrical and surface military maneuvers by the angels. These serve as a kind of ornamental frame for the sleeping couple and as a transition to the startling obscenity of Satan,

> Squat like a Toad, close at the eare of *Eve*;
> Assaying by his Devilish art to reach
> The Organs of her Fancie...   (800-802)

In their first appearance Adam and Eve have been shown as grand distant figures, then developed as private beings within the hierarchy of God's creation; finally they are shown in emblematic embrace, with the mystery of privacy flanked by the ornamental figurings of God's protection. The whole scene is made dramatically poignant and pointed by the consistent menace of Satan who finally usurps the end of Book IV. This is an example of Milton's decorum. The ambiguous potential of self is here in abundance: the sole propriety, the richness of private love. This is entwined with the hierarchical view of the Garden, the bower as benevolently created center. Satan menaces both of these values. The scene provides a reservoir of private "character" for Adam and Eve with tactful assertion of the doctrinal frame of the poem, and dramatic threat.

The opening of Book V increases the richness and the tension. Adam wakes to a conventional sunrise from a sound sleep,

> for his sleep
> Was Aerie light from pure digestion bred,   (3-4)

to find Eve in troubled sleep. She wakes and recites the dream instilled by Satan. Adam then comforts her. The episode, with which criticism has dwelt fully and sympathetically, awakens us to the full drama of danger. But the structure of the poem will place the fall later; this vivid presagement of danger is made to stay with us through the gigantic flashbacks of the War in Heaven and the Creation. The poet must sustain the memory of danger; more important he must find a way of relating the War in Heaven.

As a preliminary to the solution we have the lovely morning hymn. Milton pays close attention to the propriety of the praise of God:

> each Morning duly paid
> In various style, for neither various style
> Nor holy rapture wanted they to praise
> Thir Maker, in fit strains pronounc't or sung
> Unmeditated, such prompt eloquence
> Flowd from thir lips, in Prose or numerous Verse...
> (145-150)

This is more than antiprelatical prayer; it is *natural*. And the claim for the propriety of natural spontaneous prayer comes after Adam's comment on the dangers of Fancy, who

> misjoyning shapes,
> Wilde work produces oft, and most in dreams,
> Ill matching words and deeds long past or late.   (111-113)

This is typical, I think, of Milton's refusal to over-simplify issues in the poem.

The Hymn itself is a paean to plenitude, motion, and light. The great catalogue is in interesting rich motion which produces song. There is a remarkable linking of the images of physics with those to follow of biology. These links are effected by the very richness of the motion, reminiscent of the eccentrical equation of Heaven:

> And yee five other wandring Fires that move
> In mystic Dance not without Song, resound
> His praise, who out of Darkness call'd up Light.
> Aire, and ye Elements the eldest birth
> Of Natures Womb, that in quaternion run
> Perpetual Circle, multiform; and mix
> And nourish all things, let your ceasless change
> Varie to our great Maker still new praise.   (177-184)

This vision of complex and irregular motion is further enlivened by suggestions of spirit or breath expelled:

> Ye Mists and Exhalations that now rise
> From Hill or steaming Lake...   (185-186)

> His praise ye Winds, that from four Quarters blow,
> Breathe soft or loud   (192-193)

> Fountains and yee, that warble, as ye flow,
> Melodious murmurs, warbling tune his praise.
> Joyn voices all ye living Souls, ye Birds,
> That singing up to Heaven Gate ascend,
> Bear on your wings and in your notes his praise;
> Yee that in Waters glide, and yee that walk
> The Earth, and stately tread, or lowly creep;
> Witness if I be silent, Morn or Eeven,
> To Hill, or Valley, Fountain, or fresh shade
> Made vocal by my Song, and taught his praise.   (195-204)

The Hymn ends as one great exhalation of joyful praise, implicit with life, and moving toward the metaphor of biological wholeness.[57]

The next paragraph describes the "work" which Adam and Eve are to do. Here, the Garden is an elegant analogue to the married bliss in moral hierarchy of Adam and Eve; the couple go

> where any row
> Of Fruit-trees overwoodie reachd too farr
> Thir pamperd boughes, and needed hands to check
> Fruitless imbraces: or they led the Vine
> To wed her Elm; she spous'd about him twines
> Her mariageable arms, and with her brings
> Her dowr th' adopted Clusters, to adorn
> His barren leaves.   (212-219)

It is a richly natural, but also private and domestic, Adam and Eve now before us.

I should like here to rehearse some of my assumptions about decorum in *Paradise Lost* in preparation for an intensive reading of the breakfast in paradise scene. I should hope that the view of this scene as comedy will not seem inconsistent with the decorum I have

---

[57]   My attention was called late to Joseph Summers' brilliant essay, "Grateful Vicissitude in Paradise Lost", *PMLA*, LXIX (1954), 251-264. This essay is relevant not only to my discussion of the Morning Hymn and the Garden, but also to my discussion of Heaven. It is now available in *The Muse's Method* (Cambridge, 1962).

described. And I would hope, more importantly, that a reading under the aegis of this decorum would yield new insights into a difficult scene.

For all of its magnificent unity, *Paradise Lost* is not monolithic. Variety coexists with decorum. Indeed these two important Renaissance concepts enrich and control one another in crucial ways. Because our demands for propriety in a work of the past are stricter (or at least more constricted) than Milton's, we are likely to miss one characteristic operation of Milton's decorum – the relating in fluid, various and sometimes startling ways of the scene to the whole poem. Far from being a mere rigid consistency of diction and action, Milton's decorum is rather a delicate and complicated, an *organic*, adjustment of speech, action, character to the needs of the particular scene with, at the same time, full and resonant adherence to the demands of the whole poetic vision – the great Miltonic Christian epic.

The great Christian epic is, in fact, able to sustain even the adjustment to comedy. Our thin decorum is nervous about admitting the comic to proximity with the official sublime. Milton is more daring. Just as his prose sometimes tests the boundaries between scurrility and polemic, his poetry tests the boundaries between comic and sublime. His conception of decorum is able to contain harmonniously the magnificent and tragic and the modest and comic.

Renaissance literary theory insists that comedy concern itself with the middle class, "with the actions of private citizens, with the familiar and domestic aspect of life rather than with the affairs of state, which are the province of the tragic poet".[58] Accompanying this is the injunction that, "The diction and verse of comedy should attempt to catch the rhythms of middle-class speech".[59] These aspects of local action, character, and style are what is meant by "comic" in this analysis. The important idea that comedies begin in trouble and end in peace[60] is not engaged here, nor is the theory

[58] Vernon Hall, Jr., *Renaissance Literary Criticism* (Gloucester, Mass., 1959), p. 43.
[59] *Ibid.*, p. 44.
[60] See as an example the selections from Thomas Heywood's *An Apology for Actors* in Allen H. Gilbert, *Literary Criticism: Plato to Dryden* (New York, 1940), p. 555. See also p. 225.

that comedy castigates vice.[61] I wish to use only some of the conventional theories about comedy in arguing that a part of the great epic can be domestic, "middle-class", comic, and still closely and clearly related to the whole.

The agent of this particular exposition will be Raphael:

> Them thus imploid beheld
> With pittie Heav'ns high King, and to him call'd
> *Raphael*, the sociable Spirit, that deign'd
> To travel with *Tobias*, and secur'd
> His marriage with the seaventimes-wedded Maid. (V. 219-223)

Raphael is the "medicine of God",[62] the *sociable* spirit who *deign'd* (both condescended and thought fit) to travel with Tobias. Raphael is consistent throughout the poem; he is in Book VII, "the affable Arch-Angel" (1. 41); in Book VIII he is "Benevolent and facil" (1. 65); and in Book XI, he is remembered as "sociably mild" (1. 234). This identification and indeed imaginative classification is part of the operation of decorum.

Milton presents not only a sociable Raphael, but one who has previously been connected with comedy. It is possible that the earlier mention of Tobias, which has disturbed some critics, is a proleptic reminder of the Apocryphal Book of Tobit in which Raphael is distinctly involved in a humane comedy.

And Tobit said unto him, Brother, of what tribe and of what family art thou? Shew me. And he said unto him, Seekest thou a tribe and a family, or a hired man which shall go with thy son? And Tobit said unto him, I would know, brother, thy kindred and thy name. And he said, I am Azarias, the son of Ananias the great, of thy brethren. And he said unto him, Welcome, brother; and be not angry with me, because I sought to know thy tribe and family: and thou art my brother, of an honest and good lineage: ... But tell me, what wages shall I give thee? a drachma a day, and those things that be necessary for thee, as unto my son? And moreover, if ye return safe and sound, I will add something to thy wages

---

[61]   Nevil Coghill makes a stimulating distinction here between medieval and Renaissance comedy ("The Basis of Shakesperean Comedy", *Essay and Studies*, 1950, pp. 1-28).   Though Milton's comedy can lay claim to those aspects of Renaissance comedy I note above, in his emphasis on "joye and greet solas" he is, in *Paradise Lost*, perhaps even closer to the kind of comedy Mr. Coghill describes in his essay.

[62]   John Milton, *Complete Poems and Major Prose*, ed. Merritt Y. Hughes (New York, 1957), p. 307 n.

... but God, which dwelleth in heaven, shall prosper your journey; and may his angel go with you. And they went forth to depart, and the young man's dog with them.[63]

In Book V of *Paradise Lost* Milton first reminds us of this rich comic scene and then uses the character of Raphael to create his own kind of comedy. God instructs Raphael in his errand:

> Go therefore, half this day as friend with friend
> Converse with *Adam*, in what Bowre or shade
> Thou find'st him from the heat of Noon retir'd,
> To respit his day-labour with repast,
> Or with repose...   (229-233)

God at once circumscribes and humanizes Raphael's action in the scene: "half this day as friend with friend". The flight of Raphael is of profound significance, though even here, in God's instructions to Raphael there is a kind of humanizing of God's rhetoric, a kind of tripping indecorousness:

> left free to will,
> Left to his own free Will, his Will though free,
> Yet mutable...   (235-237)

It is as though a minor projection of the Deity had been brought forward temporarily. At the end of the speech the lines focus on Adam:

> Least wilfully transgressing he pretend
> Surprisal, unadmonisht, unforewarnd.   (244-245)

We see Adam, in the repetition of Adam's excuses; we see the 'Who, me?' gesture.

These important preliminary adjustments of decorum having been made, the scene is set in context of the whole poem by the next lines:

> So spake th' Eternal Father, and fulfilld
> All Justice...   (246-247)

The flight of Raphael to earth is one of the splendors of the poem, but the flight is more than an architectural parallel to Satan's flight. Along with the beauty of the angel and the gates is the function of the flight in focusing the scene on earth, an assertion of the *scale* of the thing:

[63] The Book of Tobit in *The Apocrypha*, rev. ed. (London, 1929), 109-110.

> As when by night the Glass
> Of *Galileo*, less assur'd, observes
> Imagind Lands and Regions in the Moon...   (261-263)

We see the earth in a glass and in contrast to the vastness of space
through which Raphael is passing:

> Down thither prone in flight
> He speeds, and through the vast Ethereal Skie
> Sailes between worlds and worlds...   (266-268)

Raphael arrives, after a journey of brilliantly varied motion, "within soare/ Of Towring Eagles" (270-271); and Milton describes his
dazzling beauty which is not only heaven-like, but literally brings
some of Heaven with him, colors and fragrance:

> Like *Maia's* son he stood,
> And shook his Plumes, that Heav'nly fragrance filld
> The circuit wide.   (285-287)

Raphael's fragrance meets those of earth:

> Into the blissful field, through Groves of Myrrhe,
> And flouring Odours, Cassia, Nard, and Balme;
> A Wilderness of sweets; for Nature here
> Wantond as in her prime, and plaid at will
> Her Virgin Fancies, pouring forth more sweet,
> Wilde above Rule or Art; enormous bliss.   (292-297)

This is a different garden from the one Milton shows in Book IV.
It is at once less formidable and wilder, a gentler and more natural
place. Another delicate adjustment of the decorum has been made,
and one means of change is the shift from the sense of sight to smell.
This is a very different garden from the archetypal one:

> the Tree of Life,
> High eminent, blooming Ambrosial Fruit
> Of vegetable Gold...   (IV. 218-220)

> from that Saphire Fount the crisped Brooks,
> Rowling on Orient Pearl and sands of Gold,
> With mazie error under pendant shades
> Ran Nectar...   (IV. 237-240)

Raphael would be less effective in the garden of Book IV, and the

Adam and Eve of domesticity and simple curiosity would be absurd.

Adam sees Raphael coming, in a passage of humane modifiers:

> Him through the *spicie* Forrest onward com
> *Adam* discernd, as *in the dore* he sat
> Of his *coole Bowre*, while now the mounted Sun
> Shot down direct his fervid Raies to warme
> Earths inmost womb, more warmth then *Adam* needs;
> And *Eve* within, due at her hour prepar'd
> For dinner *savourie* fruits, of taste to please
> True appetite, and not disrelish thirst
> Of nectarous draughts between, from milkie stream,
> Berrie or Grape...
>   (298-307) (my italics except for proper nouns)

With the exception of "nectarous", the words are all limited to the human, and not the archetypal human, scene. Even the sun sends "fervid Raies", "more warmth than Adam needs". Milton has taken the reader on an extraordinary journey downward even to the appetites. He has fused the scale, the setting, and the actors into a decorum of the wilderness of sweets. This leads on to the comedy of the breakfast scene.

Adam's first words in this "scene" are "Haste hither *Eve*" (1.308). After the tremendous flight of Raphael, speed with dignity, these words are more than gently humorous. We are in the world of man's speech, man's limited imagination. Apart from the excessive urgency, there is understatement, too, and, at the end, a kind of bumbling in the sound of "Morn/ Ris'n on mid-noon".

Adam urges Eve to prepare for their guest and she complies in words of urgency that have a "busy, busy" quality played against the stately arrival of the angel:

> But goe with speed,
> And what thy stores contain, bring forth and poure
> Abundance, fit to honour and receive
> Our Heav'nly stranger; well we may afford
> Our givers thir own gifts, and large bestow
> From large bestowd, where Nature multiplies
> Her fertil growth, and by disburd'ning grows
> More fruitful, which instructs us not to spare.
> To whom thus *Eve. Adam*, earths hallowd mould,

Of God inspir'd, small store will serve, where store,
All seasons, ripe for use hangs on the stalk;
Save what by frugal storing firmness gains
To nourish, and superfluous moist consumes:
But I will haste and from each bough and break,
Each Plant and juciest Gourd will pluck such choice
To entertain our Angel guest, as hee
Beholding shall confess that here on Earth
God hath dispenst his bounties as in Heav'n.
    So saying, with dispatchful looks in haste
She turns, on hospitable thoughts intent
What choice to chuse for delicacie best,
What order, so contriv'd as not to mix
Tastes, not well joynd, inelegant, but bring
Taste after taste upheld with kindliest change,
Bestirs her then...   (313-337)

This is comedy. Milton here adjusts the verbs to stress the disparity
between Adam and Eve and their guest. Inadequate awe; a sense of
exaggerated activity; the somewhat pompous generosity ("and by
disburd'ning grows / More fruitful"); Eve's rustic but elegant Epi-
cureanism; and the sententious and intense efficiency of the newly-
wed – all these are here in remarkable comic variety and unity.

Lines 337-349 prolong Eve's busy-ness; she gathers, heaps (with
unsparing hand), crushes, presses, tempers, strews, while Raphael
advances. The emphasis is on Eve's busy hands; the fruit is described in tactile terms: "Rough, or smooth rin'd, or bearded husk,
or shell" (this contrasts with "and without Thorn the Rose", in
Book IV, 1. 256). It is an extraordinary domestic scene with a
smoothly established constriction of scale of character, setting,
motion, and emotion. But Milton does not for long allow a foreground scene to exist independent of the epic background. Adam,
the proud young husband, goes to greet the guest:

Mean while our Primitive great Sire, to meet
His god-like Guest, walks forth, without more train
Accompani'd then with his own compleat
Perfections, in himself was all his state,
More solemn then the tedious pomp that waits
On Princes, when thir rich Retinue long
Of Horses led, and Grooms besmeard with Gold
Dazles the croud, and sets them all agape.   (350-357)

Adam and Eve, with their practical, and excessive, confrontation of the practical have held the foreground. Now the archetypal human is briefly reasserted in relation to the great frame of the epic. The scene moves on then to further consistent exploration of the comic and human. Angel and man go to the arbor which is:

> With flourets deck't and fragrant smells; but *Eve*
> Undeckt, save with her self more lovely fair
> Then Wood-Nymph, or the fairest Goddess feign'd
> Of three that in Mount *Ida* naked strove,
> Stood to entertain her guest from Heav'n; no vaile
> Shee needed, Vertue-proof, no thought infirme
> Alterd her cheek.   (379-385)

In the picture of Adam naked, Milton stressed "his own compleat/ Perfections, in himself", his real dignity compared with the false dignity of earthly pomp. In the picture of Eve naked, Milton stresses her nakedness: "Eve/ Undeckt"; the adjective is prominent by position and by contrast to "deck't". And there is much naked flesh in the picture of the three goddesses tussling over that other apple. Milton is insisting here, and insisting by involving us, on the rich beauty and, by implication, the dangers of the flesh. There is a linking here with The Fall, as the golden apple of Eris would suggest. And as Raphael's greeting suggests:

> On whom the Angel *Haile*
> Bestowd, the holy salutation us'd
> Long after to blest *Marie*, second *Eve*.
> Haile Mother of Mankind, whose fruitful Womb
> Shall fill the World more numerous with thy Sons
> Then with these various fruits the Trees of God
> Have heap'd this Table.   (385-391)

The fusion of themes is remarkable and daring. Sensuality and the annunciation, the paradox of the *felix culpa* within the comedy of fruits of trees and wombs and the potential implication of angels and readers in the nakedness of Eve. The power of the flesh over angel is developed below (ll. 443-450)[64] but only after an amusing suspension of reaction.

[64] The question of Eve's effect on Raphael is subtly raised again in Book VIII:
> "And from about her shot Darts of desire
> Into all Eyes to wish her still in sight.

Angel and man arrive at the table genially described. Then comes one of the genuinely *achieved* comic lines in English:

> A while discourse they hold;
> No fear lest Dinner coole...

The line has disturbed a long series of influential readers: Addison, Tennyson, Taine among others.[65] And the history of the line is almost a history of the understanding of Milton's decorum. Milton exploits the naturalness of the scene and the supernaturalness of the angel, as God's representative, to create a comic disparity. The decorum of Milton's exquisite scenic adjustments has made possible the comedy. And the comedy will make possible a larger decorum, the very propriety of "natural" in the poem. It is a kind of interactment that only poetry can achieve. The key figure is Raphael with his ambivalent character: sociable; a friend of Tobit's; and glorious. Raphael's role here is as a mediator between the natural and supernatural. His great speech on hierarchy is part of his function, but perhaps more important even is his speech on transubstantiation; and that is made possible and effective only by the kind of scene in which Adam, Eve and Raphael have just participated.

Before partaking, Raphael informs Adam that both men and angels contain

> Within them every lower facultie
> Of sense, whereby they hear, see, smell, touch, taste,
> Tasting concoct, digest, assimilate,
> And corporeal to incorporeal turn.   (410-413)

The consistency of Milton's angelology is not easily established. Robert West suggests that the angelic eating is a striking prop to Milton's larger concern for the wholeness of man and for "the

---

And *Raphael* now to *Adam's* doubt propos'd
Benevolent and facil thus repli'd".   (ll. 62-65)
Part of this emphasis, of course, is to contrast Raphael's "Love unlibidinous" with Satan's jealous lust.

[65] Addison, *Spectator* No. 275, regards this as a lapse into "idiomatic Ways of Speaking". Tennyson calls it "a terrible bathos"; see Hallam Tennyson, *Alfred Lord Tennyson: A Memoir by His Son* (New York, 1897), p. 520: And Taine enjoys an extended joke about Adam and Eve as "domesticated". *History of English Literature*, trans. by N. Van Laun (New York, 1895), pp. 541, 543, 549.

stages of nature's scale as a sort of telescoping succession in which
the higher comprehends the lower and the whole of the lower may be
transplanted into the higher".[66] More consistent than the angelology is the comedy. Lines 412-414 have a compressed rhythmic mo-
notony with a widened out conclusion, all of which suggests the explanation "tossed off".[67] The paradox of the comic-natural working
with the epic-supernatural is surely closer to the end of Milton's
strenuous and subtle skill here than is the uneasily held view of
C. S. Lewis:

When his Archangel dines with Adam he did not simply appear to eat ...
Real hunger preceded, real assimilation, with a consequent rise of temp-
erature, accompanied the meal. It is inconceivable that Milton should
have so emphasized the reality of angelic nourishment (and even angelic
excretion) if the bodies he attributed to his angels were merely a poetical
device. The whole passage becomes intelligible, and much less poetically
grotesque, when we realize that Milton put it there chiefly because he
thought it *true*. In this he did not stand alone.[68]

But Mr. West's studies suggest that Milton's handling of this scene
is not clearly traditional, that indeed it creates problems.[69] Perhaps here it is a mistake to impose a body of data on a passage to
which the imagination has been closed, attempting by this imposition to render the passage "less poetically grotesque". An acceptance of Milton's suggestions, in his adjustments of setting, character, and action, in short of decorum, would enable the reader to see
these words of the friendly angel as humorous:[70]

> and to taste
> Think not I shall be nice.   (432-433)

The eating itself is done with humorous gusto:

[66]   Robert H. West, *Milton and the Angels* (Athens, 1955), p. 168.
[67]   This kind of bare, thumping cataloguing is more obviously comic in Book
III, ll. 474-75: "Embryo's and Idiots, Eremits and Friers / White, Black and
Grey, with all thir trumperie".
[68]   C. S. Lewis, *A Preface to Paradise Lost* (Oxford, 1954), p. 106.
[69]   "Perhaps Milton has shown in his lines on angels' eating and making love a
certain obduracy; he has insisted on giving answers that his plot did not demand
to questions that it did not urgently raise". West, *op. cit.*, p. 173.
[70]   David Daiches is one of the few who does this scene some justice. See his
Milton, p. 197.

> So down they sat,
> And to thir viands fell, nor seemingly
> The Angel, nor in mist, the common gloss
> Of Theologians...   (433-436)

At the end of the real meal (not like the one in the mist of Tobit)[71] Raphael answers Adam's questions on nourishment with the second of his Chain of Being speeches (the first was 415-429). This is a brilliant ascending passage that leads to a climactic linking of angels and man:

> So from the root
> Springs lighter the green stalk, from thence the leaves
> More aerie, last the bright consummate floure
> Spirits odorous breathes: flours and thir fruit
> Mans nourishment, by gradual scale sublim'd
> To vital Spirits aspire, to animal,
> To intellectual, give both life and sense,
> Fansie and understanding, whence the Soule
> Reason receives, and reason is her being,
> Discursive, or Intuitive; discourse
> Is oftest yours, the latter most is ours,
> Differing but in degree, of kind the same.   (479-490)

This passage soars higher than the other on Chain of Being; one is a description in terms of nourishment, the other in terms of essence. In its range, this passage has begun to pull Raphael upward and away from the limited domestic scene; and Raphael is taking Adam and Eve with him. Two practicing human beings and *the* sociable angel have had breakfast. Now they are being drawn to different roles. But not before a fusion of the natural and appetitive, and the supernatural:

> Wonder not then, what God for you saw good
> If I refuse not, but convert, as you,
> To proper substance, time may come when men
> With Angels may participate, and find
> No inconvenient Diet, nor too light Fare:
> And from these corporal nutriments perhaps
> Your bodies may at last turn all to Spirit,
> Improv'd by tract of time, and wingd ascend
> Ethereal, as wee, or may at choice

---

[71] *The Apocrypha*, p. 118.

> Here or in Heav'nly Paradises dwell;
> If ye be found obedient...   (491-501)

The decorous comedy of the angelic eating has become the means to a symbol of God's plan. And in the dazzling conceit, "Improv'd by tract of time",[72] the eternal transubstantiation – digestion, and reunion with God – the guiding metaphor of the scene is explicitly related to the poem.

The breakfast scene is over and Raphael in a more formal way begins to transact God's business. His next address to Adam is as "Son of Heav'n and Earth" (1. 519). Adam and Eve become again the archetypal primitive great parents. But the dramatic potentialities of the couple have been immeasurably increased by this view of them. And so have the "theological" potentialities of man. Probably most important, the dramatic possibility of sustained metaphor has been introduced. The "what if" of angelic nourishment has become a medium for exploring man's spiritual future, the relation of his limited "comic" self to his potential. Raphael will say "what if" again:

> and what surmounts the reach
> Of human sense, I shall delineate so,
> By lik'ning spiritual to corporal forms,
> As may express them best, though what if Earth
> Be but the shaddow of Heav'n, and things therein
> Each to other like, more then on Earth is thought?
>   (V. 571-576)

And he will show the War in Heaven and Creation as sustained metaphor.[73] In the Garden, Raphael has used the metaphor of digestion as order; it is at once singularly appropriate and charming-

---

[72] William G. Madsen misses the point when he says of this passage: "This is the familiar Neoplatonic doctrine of the vertical ascent through the scale of being, not the horizontal journey through "tract of time" that fallen mankind will have to make".

And the kind of typological reading of the poem which he gives does not seem to me as fully answerable to the poem's complexities as my "imaginative" or "poetic" reading. See William G. Madsen, "Earth the Shadow of Heaven: Typological Symbolism in Paradise Lost", *PMLA*, LXXV (Dec. 1960), p. 523. The quotation marks around "imaginitive" and "poetic" are quoted from Mr. Madsen's note on p. 525.

[73] VII, 113-14.

ly ingenious. For Milton digestion is an orderly disposition, used often by him metaphorically, as in the *Christian Doctrine* where he speaks of matter being "adorned and digested into order by the hand of God".[74]

Supply and brilliantly Milton's picture of Adam and Eve in the garden expands and contracts in a kind of systolic decorum of the needs of the subject. The initial grandeur of our primitive great parents becomes qualified by their privacy. Their simple comic humanity is expressed through the mediation of the sociable angel and breakfast. Raphael then leads Adam and Eve back to grandeur and responsibility toward the end of Book V.

Later in the poem, Milton himself directs us again toward this kind of reading of the breakfast scene; he reminds us of the purposeful shift in style and action. At the beginning of Book IX, in preparing for the Fall, he refers back in contrast to the scene just examined:

> No more of talk where God or Angel Guest
> With Man, as with his Friend, familiar us'd
> To sit indulgent, and with him partake
> Rural repast, permitting him the while
> Venial discourse unblam'd: I now must change
> Those Notes to Tragic...

Milton's decorum is not monolithic. It adapts to subject, or rather it is the medium through which the subject adapts the materials of the poem. Milton's decorum is so comprehensive that it includes meaningfully a great richness and variety. The humanity and humor are in the poem: they do not have to be ignored. The human and comic are richly, tightly integrated with the epic in a demonstration of Milton's concept of decorum.

---

[74] Columbia *Milton*, XV, 23. Digestion and concoction, a near synonym, are common metaphors for order in Milton. See the Columbia *Milton*. For *digestion*, III, 225; III, 453; XVI, 195; for *concoction* III, 225. The *NED* gives as one definition for digestion, "To dispose methodically or according to a system; to reduce into a systematic form, usually with condensation; to classify". And it quotes Bishop Hall as using the word to mean, "To settle and arrange methodically in the mind; to consider, think, or ponder over".

AFTERWORD

I have tried to argue for a whole Milton, a poet whose "harmonical and ingenious soul did lodge in a beautiful and well-proportioned body". I am not arguing about the man, though I have tried to use his attitudes toward personal wholeness as an analogy and director toward the visionary unity in the prose and verse.

I take my warrant for concern with the Milton image and redefinition of it from the abuse of that image in much modern criticism, the imposition of the flawed and monstrously willful John Milton on his prose and verse, and the consequent misreading of his works. If I appear to err for the whole man as egregiously as Mr. Waldock for a bifurcated one, I can only say that I have pointed to the evidence of the verse and prose, not to the "reputation"; and I would wish to stand or fall on my readings.

The operation of decorum that Plato suggests in his emphasis on the proper functioning of parts in a whole has, I hope, been demonstrated in *Paradise Lost*, where the local brilliance of the scenes in Hell reaches its natural limits and expires. And the Aristotelian sense of a pulsating decorum, the systolic expansion and contraction of the verse to the needs of the poem, should be clearly relevant and instructive in reading the scenes in the Garden. I hope that both Aristophanes and Erasmus suggest some warrant for Milton's extraordinary freedom, not only in the prose – the vehement expressions and grim laughter of his left hand – but in the epic, in the austerity of Book III, the sensuousness of Book IV, the comedy of Book V. "I a Christian must speak to Christians about the Christian religion". The epic can be read with a continuing awareness of Western traditions of unity-with-variety; these traditions are different from, and I think greater than, ideas of rhetorical conformity. I have given only steps in my reading of *Paradise Lost*, though these steps should suggest a complete reading of the poem. The kind of energies and return which I have tried to show in Heaven would I think be found in the Creation and in the pre-lapsarian Garden. The kind of extended comic metaphor that Milton uses for the breakfast scene can be applied to the War in Heaven, and I hope that the metaphor of digestion can be viewed sympathetically as one of the major metaphors in the poem. The critical and continuous adjustments and circumscriptions, expansions and perspectives of *Paradise Lost* are just the concern of a student of decorum. It is a flaw of that concept that it comes so close to meaning a total reading; I would hope that a little charity will operate toward a brief study which approaches that claim.

But Milton's decorum *is* something like organic unity: it raises the image of that unity and then proceeds to close up truth to truth. This ideal goes hand in hand with the procedure, the end with the means. Working chiefly from the *Paradise Lost*, Professor Joseph Summers has arrived at a similar conclusion:

Whatever Milton may have thought earlier, by the time he came to write *Paradise Lost* he seems to have reached the general enlightened conclusion that literary decorum could not be judged apart from the materials and aims of the particular literary work. Decorum concerned the proper relations between the parts and the whole, the propriety of means and ends. The "decorous" in this sense, like our modern "functional", implies that beautiful detail must contribute to or reflect the whole; but unlike the modern word, Milton's term also implies that harmony is natural to man and that man is more than the sum of his activities. It was precisely this sense of the *harmonious* whole which required that *Paradise Lost* should continuously challenge the abstracted and conventional decorums of the past. The parts and the whole of this poem must be proper for the end of celebrating the ways of God and of human history, those ways which have violated the sense of decorum of most civilizations, most literatures, most ruling classes, and most men.[1]

Mr. Summers has stated elegantly what, it seems to me, is the most important aspect of Milton's whole work. The ideal of unity and

---

[1] *The Muses Method* (Cambridge, 1962), p. 21. I came to Mr. Summers' fine book after I had finished the main body of my study.

the means of attaining it are everywhere in Milton. He presents it in soaring images of the poet or the married couple or the military leader, or the heavenly choir, or the abstracts Truth, the Commonwealth, education; or he implies it in his violent attacks on spurious unity, on insincerity, on superficiality, on thinness or incompleteness in religion, in language, in *feeling*; he implies it in Satan, in Belial, in Eve fallen, in the landscape of Hell. Always the unity he idealizes and works toward is that of the richly realized individual in a universe of God's making.

I think our failures with Milton are largely failures to read with his decorum. The faint demur of Mr. Eliot has, one suspects, its roots not so much in a greater respect for the natural man but in a lesser. It is the ambition and the richness of the claims for the whole self that make much modern criticism suspicious of Milton. Not believing in such a thing as the significant whole man, how can we read these magnificent claims for him as anything but silly, pompous, in bad *taste*: one doesn't write long ambitious poems about wholeness. In an era when *The Wasteland* was everybody's theme song, it is little wonder that the Adam and Eve of Book IV seemed a kind of incredible mistake perpetrated on literary history by a willful Puritan and academic inertia. One part of modern criticism rejected Milton's claims for the human identity itself.

One part rejected that human identity as related to God and found the responsibilities of that relationship inhuman. Critics like Mr. Waldock and Mr. Peter wanted God the Father to be just plain Dad, though sometimes confusing matters by arguing that God was *too* human. Professor Waldock substituted a system of "human relations" for the man-god relationship and worked strictly within that context. It became a critical commonplace that Milton had not written a great poem, that the *Paradise Lost* could not possibly have been a great poem. We have had, and continue to have, bravish denials that *Paradise Lost* is an epic poem as Milton describes it. But the denial comes from those who reject, even as a poetic possibility, one or other factor of the fierce equation, the idea of man as a whole or the idea of God. The disintegrators have, happily, been able to use each other to prove their points.

The idea of Man and the idea of God; it would be easier simply to say Christian Humanism and to say it firmly and repeatedly as Professor Douglas Bush does in one of the best books on Milton. Perhaps I have been elaborately avoiding the term, because I can not say the first word with the fervor of Professor Bush or C. S. Lewis. But one must insist on the idea, in the complicated, exciting but finally unified sense in which a John Milton could conceive it, as the source of the decorum of *Paradise Lost* and, though I have not engaged them here, of *Samson Agonistes* and *Paradise Regained.*

One wants to say more than that the idea of Man in relationship to God is the proper historical context for reading John Milton. But, for us, the artist must make the statement of faith. Too self-conscious, too embarrassed to say Man-in-God, we turn to John Milton and to the richly continuing tradition of Western literature.

LIST OF WORKS CITED

Adams, Joseph Quincy, ed., *Chief Pre-Shakespearean Dramas* (Boston, 1924).

Addison, Joseph, *The Works of the Right Honourable Joseph Addison*, ed. Richard Hurd, Vol. XXX (London, 1856).

Allen, Don Cameron, *The Harmonious Vision* (Baltimore, 1954).

The Apocrypha, rev. ed. (London, 1929).

Aristophanes, *Comedies*, 2 vols. (New York, 1931).

Aristotle, *The Rhetoric and Poetics of Aristotle*, ed. Friedrich Solmsen *(The Modern Library)* (New York, 1954).

Atkins, J. W. H., *English Literary Criticism: The Medieval Phase* (London, 1952).

——, *Literary Criticism in Antiquity*, 2 vols. (London, 1952).

Augustine, "Christian Instruction", in *The Fathers of the Church*, Vol. II (New York, 1947).

——, *The City of God*, transl. Marcus Dods *(The Modern Library)* (New York, 1950).

Barker, Arthur E., *Milton and the Puritan Dilemma* (Toronto, 1942).

——, "Seven Types of Milton Criticism", *University of Toronto Quarterly*, 25 (1956), 494-506.

Bergonzi, Bernard, "Criticism and the Milton Controversy", in *The Living Milton*, ed., Frank Kermode (London, 1960).

Bourne, E. C. E., *The Anglicanism of William Laud* (London, 1947).

Broadbent, J. B., "Milton's Rhetoric", *Modern Philology*, LVI (May, 1959), 224-242.

Burton, Henry, *A Reply to a Relation of the Conference Betweene William Laude and Mr. Fisher the Jesuite* (London, 1640).

Calvin, John, *Institutes of the Christian Religion*, transl. John Allen, Vol. II (Philadelphia, n.d.).

Certain Briefe Treatises, Written by Diverse Learned Men ... (Oxford, 1641).

Chaucer, Geoffrey, *The Poetical Works of Chaucer*, ed. F. N. Robinson (Cambridge, 1933).

Cicero, *Ad C. Herennium: De Ratione Dicendi (Rhetorica ad Herennium)*, transl. Harry Caplan *(The Loeb Classical Library)* (London, 1954).

——, *Brutus* and *Orator*, transl. G. L. Hendrickson and A. M. Hubbell *(The Loeb Classical Library)* (Cambridge, 1952).

——, *Cicero's Three Books of Offices or Moral Duties*, transl. Cyrus R. Edmonds (New York, 1871).

Clark, Donald Lemen, *John Milton at St. Paul's School* (New York, 1948).

Coghill, Nevill, "The Basis of Shakespearean Comedy", *Essays ana Studies* (1950), pp. 1-28.

Cornford, Francis MacDonald, ed., *The Republic of Plato* (New York, 1954).

Crane, W. G., *Wit and Rhetoric in the Renaissance* (New York, 1948).

Daiches, David, *Milton* (London, 1957).

Danielou, Jean, *Origen*, transl. Walter Mitchell (New York, 1955).

A Defence of the Humble Remonstrance Against the frivolous and false exceptions of Smectymnuus (London, 1641).

Diels, Hermann, *Die Fragmente der Vorsokratiker* (Berlin, 1922).

Dionysius of Halicarnassus, *On Literary Composition*, transl. and ed. W. Rhys Roberts (London, 1910).

——, *The Three Literary Letters*, transl. W. Rhys Roberts (Cambridge, 1901).

Edelstein, Ludwig, "The Function of the Myth in Plato's Philosophy", *Journal of the History of Ideas*, X (October, 1949), 463-480.

Empson, William, *Milton's God* (London, 1961).

——, "The Satan of Milton", *Hudson Review*, XII (Spring, 1960), 33-59.

Ferry, Anne Davidson, *Milton's Epic Voice* (Cambridge, Mass., 1963).

Freeman, Kathleen, *The Pre-Socratic Philosophers* (Cambridge, 1946).

Frye, Roland Mushat, *God, Man and Satan* (Princeton, 1960).

——, "The Teachings of Classical Puritanism on Conjugal Love", *Studies in the Renaissance*, II (1955), 148-159.

Gilbert, Allen H., *Literary Criticism: Plato to Dryden* (New York, 1940).

Hall, Joseph, *Works*, ed. Peter Hall, 12 vols. (London, 1837).

Hall, Vernon, Jr., *Renaissance Literary Criticism* (Gloucester, Mass., 1959).

Haller, William, "Hail Wedded Love", *ELH*, XIII (June, 1946), 79-97.

——, ed., *Tracts on Liberty in the Puritan Revolution*, 3 vols. (New York,1933).

——, and Malleville, "The Puritan Art of Love", *The Huntington Library Quarterly*, V (January, 1942), 235-272.

Hanford, James Holly, *John Milton, Englishman* (New York, 1949).

Hendrickson, G. L., "The Origin and Meaning of the Ancient Characters of Style", *American Journal of Philology*, XXVI (1905), 249-290.

——, "The Peripatetic Mean of Style and the Three Stylistic Characters", *American Journal of Philology*, XXV (1904), 36-72.

Herbert, George, *The Works of George Herbert*, ed. F. E. Hutchinson (Oxford, 1953).

Ideal Commonwealths, ed. Henry Morley, 8th ed. (London, 1899).

Jaeger, Werner, *Paideia: The Ideals of Greek Culture*, transl. Gilbert Highet, Vol. I (New York, 1943).

Jebb, R. C., *The Attic Orators from Antiphon to Isaeus*, 2 vols. (London, 1876).

John of Salisbury, *Metalogicon*, transl. Daniel D. McGarry (Berkeley, 1955).

Kranidas, Thomas, "Milton and the Rhetoric of Zeal", *Texas Studies in Literature and Language*, VI (Winter, 1965).

——, "Milton's 'grand master peece'", *American Notes & Queries*, II (1963), 54-55.

Langdon, Ida, *Milton's Theory of Poetry and Fine Art* (New Haven, 1924).

Lattimore, Richmond, *The Odes of Pindar* (Chicago, 1945).

Laud, William, *A Relation of the Conference between ... Laud ... and Mr. Fisher the Jesuite ...*, 2nd ed. (London, 1639).

Laud, William, *A Speech Delivered in the Starr-Chamber... Concerning pretended innovations in the Church* (London, 1637).

Lewis, C. S., *A Preface to "Paradise Lost"* (Oxford, 1954).

MacCaffrey, Isabel Gamble, *Paradise Lost as 'Myth'* (Cambridge, 1959).

Madsen, William G., "Earth the Shadow of Heaven: Typological Symbolism in *Paradise Lost*", *PMLA*, LXXV (Dec., 1960).

Milton, John, *Complete Poems and Major Prose*, ed. Merritt Y. Hughes (New York, 1957).

——, *Of Reformation*, ed. Will T. Hale (New Haven and London, 1916).

——, *Prose Selections*, ed. Merritt Y. Hughes (New York, 1947).

——, *Complete Prose Works of John Milton*, ed. by several hands, 2 vols. (New Haven, 1953—).

——, *The Works of John Milton*, ed. Frank Allen Patterson *et al.*, 18 vols. (New York, 1931-1938).

Nettleship, Richard Lewis, *Lectures on the Republic of Plato* (London, 1951).

Parker, William Riley, *Milton's Contemporary Reputation* (Columbus, 1940).

Patrides, C. A., "*Paradise Lost* and the Theory of Accomodation", *Texas Studies in Literature and Language*, V (Spring, 1963).

Peter, John, *A Critique of Paradise Lost* (New York, 1960).

Plato, *The Dialogues of Plato*, transl. Benjamin Jowett, Vol. III (Oxford, 1953).

Prynne, William, *Lords Bishops* (London, 1640).

Rajan, B., *Paradise Lost and the Seventeenth Century Reader* (New York, 1948).

Roberts, W. Rhys, ed., *Aristotle The Poetics "Longinus" On the Sublime Demetrius On Style*, transl. W. Hamilton Fyfe and W. Rhys Roberts (*The Loeb Classical Library*) (Cambridge, 1953).

——, *Greek Rhetoric and Literary Criticism* (New York, 1928).

Ross, Malcolm M., *Milton's Royalism* (Ithaca, 1943).

Samuel, Irene, "The Dialogue in Heaven: A Reconsideration of Paradise Lost, III-1-417", *PMLA*, LXXII (September, 1957), 601-611.

——, *Plato and Milton* (Ithaca, 1947).

Schonlau, Sister Mary Grace, "A Study of the Language of Eloquence and the Principles of Decorum, Verisimilitude and Imitation in the Plays of George Chapman", Unpublished Ph. D. dissertation (St. Louis University, 1959).

Scott, Izora, *Controversies over the Imitation of Cicero*, (New York, 1910).

Seebohm, Frederic, *The Oxford Reformers* (London, 1896).

Shakespeare, William, *The Complete Plays and Poems of William Shakespeare*, ed. William Allan Neilson and Charles Jarvis Hill (Boston, 1942).

[SMECTYMNUUS.] *An Answer to a Book Entituled An Humble Remonstrance* (London, 1641).

Smith, G. Gregory, *Elizabethan Critical Essays*, 2 vols. (London, 1904).

Smith, James Harry and Parks, Edd Winfield, *The Great Critics* (New York, 1939).

Spencer, Hazelton, ed., *Elizabethan Plays* (Boston, 1933).

Spingarn, J. E., ed., *Critical Essays of the Seventeenth Century*, 3 vols. (Bloomington, 1957).

——, *Literary Criticism in the Renaissance* (New York, 1949).

Stein, Arnold, *Answerable Style* (Minneapolis, 1953).

——, *Donne's Lyrics: The Eloquence of Action* (Minneapolis, 1962).

——, *Heroic Knowledge* (Minneapolis, 1957).

Summers, Joseph, "Grateful Vicissitude in Paradise Lost", *PMLA*, LXIX (1954), 251-264.

——, *The Muse's Method* (Cambridge, Mass., 1962).

Svendsen, Kester, "Epic Address and Reference and the Principle of Decorum in Paradise Lost", *Philological Quarterly*, XXVIII (January, 1949), 185-206.

——, *Milton and Science* (Cambridge, 1956).

——, "Milton's *Pro Se Defensio* and Alexander More", *Texas Studies in Literature and Language*, I (Spring, 1959), 11-29.

——, "Science and Structure in Milton's Doctrine of Divorce", *PMLA*, LXVII (1952), 435-445.

Taine, H. A., *History of English Literature*, transl. N. Van Laun (New York, 1895).

Tennyson, Hallam, *Alfred Lord Tennyson: A Memoir by His Son* (New York, 1897).

Tillyard, E. M. W., *Milton* (London, 1951).

Tuve, Rosemond, *Elizabethan and Metaphysical Imagery* (Chicago, 1947).

——, *Images and Themes in Five Poems by Milton* (Cambridge, Mass., 1957).

Waldock, A. J. A., *Paradise Lost and its Critics* (Cambridge, 1959).

West, Robert H., *Milton and the Angels* (Athens, Georgia, 1955).

Wilson, Thomas, *A Christian Dictionary* (London, 1616).

Wimsatt, William K., Jr. and Brooks, Cleanth, *Literary Criticism: A Short History* (New York, 1957).

Woodhouse, A. S. P., "Nature and Grace in *The Faerie Queene*", *ELH*, XVI (1949), 194-228.

INDEX

STUDIES IN ENGLISH LITERATURE

Out:

MOUTON & CO. — PUBLISHERS — THE HAGUE